REUVEN RUBIN

REUVEN RUBIN, 1893-

Sarah Wilkinson

by

c.1

HARRY N. ABRAMS, INC. PUBLISHERS NEW YORK

Frontispiece:

1 SELF-PORTRAIT IN RED SWEATER. 1938.
Oil on canvas, 46 × 35 ½″.
Collection Ariella Rubin, Tel Aviv

Margaret L. Kaplan   *Managing Editor*

Nai Y. Chang   *Vice-President, Design*

James Wageman   *Book Design*

LIBRARY OF CONGRESS CATALOGING IN PUBLICATION DATA

Rubin, Reuven, 1893–
  Reuven Rubin.
  Bibliography : p. 283-287.
    1.   Rubin, Reuven, 1893–
I.   Wilkinson, Sarah. II. Title.
N7279. R82W54   759.95694 [B]   71–166215
ISBN 0–8109–0463–2

288p. ill.

Library of Congress Catalogue Card Number : 71–166215
Harry N. Abrams, Incorporated, New York
Printed and bound in Japan

CONTENTS

PLATES

*Colorplates are marked with an asterisk**

REUVEN RUBIN

JOY'S SOUL LIES IN THE DOING

SHAKESPEARE   *Troilus and Cressida*

2 JACOB WRESTLING WITH THE ANGEL;
KING DAVID ENTERS JERUSALEM;
ELIJAH ASCENDING TO HEAVEN
IN A CHARIOT OF FIRE. 1970.
Stained glass, three panels, each 18′ × 5′9″
Window in residency of the President
of Israel, Jerusalem

IN 1969, Reuven Rubin was commissioned to design three stained-glass windows for the reception hall of the new residency of the President of Israel under construction in Jerusalem (plates 2, 3). It was a big project, and at the time Rubin was approaching his seventy-sixth year, a period of life in which new challenges are seldom welcome. But, characteristically for him, both as an artist for whom experimenting with a new technique has always offered a stimulus to his creativity and as a man of restless energy and imagination, he accepted the commission with delight. The windows, he declared, would be his gift to the nation. Again characteristically, he took his theme from the Bible, the book that has always meant most to him and whose figures have so often been the subject of his paintings. He chose three "visions": Elijah ascending to heaven in a chariot of fire (plate 4); Jacob wrestling with the angel; and David's entry into Jerusalem, based on a text from Psalm 122: "Our feet shall stand within thy gates, O Jerusalem."

During the same period, his mind was occupied with selecting chapters from the Bible that would provide themes for three series of lithographs—*The Story of King*

3 Rubin with Israeli President Zalman Shazar discussing the stained-glass window for the new residency in Jerusalem, 1969

4 ELIJAH ASCENDING TO HEAVEN
IN A CHARIOT OF FIRE.
1969. Gouache, 24 × 17 ½″.
Design for stained-glass windows
in residency of the
President of Israel, Jerusalem

5 Rubin in his Tel Aviv studio

David, The Prophets, and *Visions of the Bible*—commissioned by various international publishers (plates 6–14).

Rubin believes that the artist is an enviable human being, the possessor of a deep source of happiness, and it is this conviction that finds expression in his paintings, with their feeling of serenity, rhythmical design, and beguiling color. Unlike many contemporary painters, he does not see in nature dark forces inimical to man, nor is he interested in trying to convey the unhappy spirit of our troubled times or to depict the sophistications of a technological age. He can say with Matisse that he dreams of "an art that is balanced, pure, and calm, free from disturbing subject matter,"[1] and he has often been quoted as saying, "I paint what I love: my family, my country, my people." These are the themes to which he has constantly returned over the years, never abandoning representation, but taking from nature only those aspects that suit his particular poetical conception of reality.

RUBIN was born in the Danube city of Galatz in Rumania on November 13, 1893, to Joel and Fanny Zelicovici. His mother, the daughter of a rabbi, was a kindly, bustling woman, completely absorbed by her family. His father, commonly known as "Reb Joel" because he spent most of his time acting as gabbai (chief synagogue official) of one of the many small synagogues in the Jewish quarter where they lived, was never able to earn an adequate living for his large family of thirteen children. Relief from the general drabness of the ghetto life was provided only by the Jewish festivals, when the family changed into less shabby clothes and a white cloth appeared on the table. But the atmosphere in the home was warm and loving, and the father, a light-haired, handsome man, had a beautiful singing voice, which he took great pleasure in using in the synagogue services and in Hassidic song. Doubtless Rubin's love of music, which he retains to this day, was engendered in childhood by the sound of his father's voice. An evening spent listening to Beethoven, Chopin, or Mozart always sends the painter back to his easel refreshed in spirit and with a renewed impetus to work.

As so often happens in a family of many children, the younger ones were precocious, and Rubin, the eighth child, was only three years old when he was sent alone to heder, the Jewish religious school. It was then that he made his first drawing, scratching out the profile of his bespectacled teacher with a piece of broken glass on

Drawings for *Visions of the Bible,*
portfolio of lithographs published by
Harry N. Abrams, Inc., New York.
1970. Pen and ink and pastel, 25 × 19″

6 GENESIS 3:23, 24. "Therefore the Lord God sent him forth from the
garden of Eden, to till the ground from whence he was taken.
"So he drove out the man; and he placed at the east of the garden of Eden
Cherubims, and a flaming sword which turned every way, to keep the way of
the tree of life."

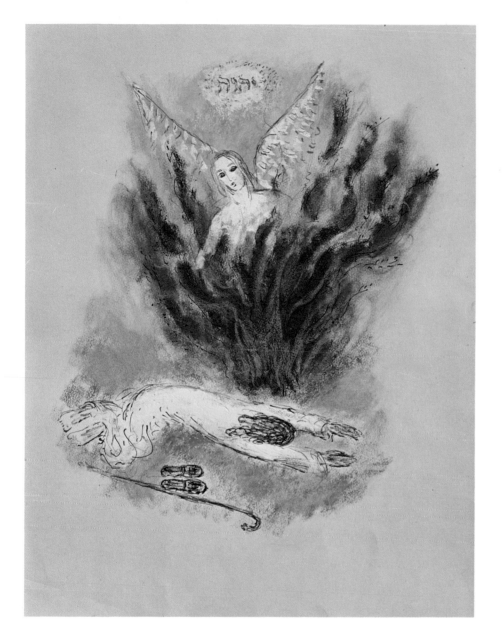

7 EXODUS 3:2. "And the angel of the Lord appeared unto him in a flame of fire out of the midst of a bush: and he looked, and, behold, the bush burned with fire, and the bush was not consumed."

8 ZECHARIAH 6:1, 5. "And I turned, and lifted up mine eyes, and looked, and, behold, there came four chariots out from between two mountains; and the mountains were mountains of brass.

"And the angel answered and said unto me, These are the four spirits of the heavens, which go forth from standing before the Lord of all the earth."

23

a brick covered with white plaster. All children like to draw, but what was unusual was that this child could produce a recognizable likeness. He recalls that he used to cover with drawings the walls of the house, freshly whitewashed for Passover holiday; understandably, he got a thrashing for this temerity.

Especially exciting to the small boy were the visits of the emissaries from Palestine, who came to Rumania on fund-raising missions. He would creep from his hiding place behind the stove to listen to their stories of the Holy Land. Carried away by their own words, they would describe a land of perpetual sunshine with every man sitting beneath his own fig tree and the young people singing and dancing in the streets in the Rejoicing of the Law (a celebration occurring on the last day of the Feast of Tabernacles). Little wonder that even as a child, Rubin dreamed of one day living in this enchanted land of his ancestors.

So sharply are the events of his early life etched on Rubin's memory that seventy years later he can speak of them as if they happened yesterday. That he associated beauty and dignity with the Jewish festivals and that his father, the most important figure in his young life, was imposing in stature and appearance, have profoundly influenced the way he depicts Jewish subjects. Not for him the pathetic, undersized creatures of the East European ghetto so often painted by others of his faith and of similar background; Rubin's figures are always marked by a certain nobility, evoking Biblical characters.

While still a youngster, he became conscious of the gulf that separated him from the rest of his family. He rebelled against the narrowness and crippling poverty of his life, while the family accepted these as inescapable facts. He was anxious for knowledge and dreamed of a wider world. Their closed existence, bounded by a rigid orthodoxy, seemed to satisfy them, but he felt within himself forces that were struggling for release. He took the difficult steps for admission to a government high school and was the first of his brothers and sisters to be able to read and write Rumanian. (The language of the household was Yiddish.) After two unhappy years at the school, where, although a good pupil and also known as "the boy who can draw," he was plagued by his anti-Semitic classmates and teachers, he was given an unusual chance to enter the Jewish High School as a non-paying pupil. For the first time he began to feel less isolated, and he made friends with boys of his own age who were not afraid of being Jews. But after reaching the fourth grade there, he left to go to work. The family was still bitterly poor and, although not yet fifteen, he had to make a contribution to the household budget. The father of a friend owned a wineshop and Rubin was engaged to work in the office, the first of many jobs he was to accept before settling down to his lifework, painting. He did manage to sell some of his sketches to a local paper, but the sums received as payment were negligible.

Increased difficulties in making ends meet made the father move his family to Falticeni, the rural town in the northern part of Moldavia where he had been born and where his mother and many relatives still lived. For the first time Rubin traveled by train and took the opportunity to stop in Jassy, the most important town in Rumania after Bucharest. It was here that he went inside an art school for the first time, his curiosity aroused when he saw that an exhibition of students' work was being held. To this day he remembers the envy with which he regarded the young students, as well as his inner determination that one day he too would study art and make painting his career.

Falticeni, with its green fields, its lake, and its trees, brought a feeling of peace to the youngster's questing mind. His job was taking the cow and goat to the meadows, where he would lie under a tree sketching or reading. The Bible became his daily companion, until its stories and figures were more real to him than the actual life he was leading. He also read everything he could lay his hands on about Theodor Herzl and his plan for the return of the Jews to Palestine and about the growing Zionist movement, for taking ever stronger root in his heart was the resolve that he also would go to Palestine, break away from the torpor of his present existence, and become an artist in a Jewish land. It seemed the dream of a fantasy-filled youth, but it was one that never let him rest. When he was seventeen, he received a letter from Vienna. The writer said he had seen some drawings of Rubin's at a Zionist congress and wished to buy them, enclosing two gold coins in payment. Rubin had no recollection of having sent any drawings to the congress and could only conclude that one of his schoolmates had done so. The writer also suggested that Rubin go to Jerusalem and study art at the Bezalel School of Arts and Crafts, which had been established by Professor Boris Schatz in 1906. It all seemed very strange, as if the hand of God were in it. His family took a more prosaic view. It was very nice to receive two gold coins, but the money would not take him very far. As for studying art and

15 MY GRANDFATHER. 1910.
Oil on cardboard, 12 × 10″.
The Rubin Museum Foundation

16 Rubin in Jerusalem, 1912

becoming an artist, this idea was simply incomprehensible to them. It was not a profession for a Jewish boy reared in strict orthodoxy. But the compulsion that talent imposes on the gifted was working in him, and when, a few weeks later, he received a letter from Professor Schatz accepting him as a student, the youngster's course was set. To Palestine he would go. He sold his old bicycle, and, with his two gold coins, he had the money to travel.

It was about this time that he painted his first portrait in oils. His maternal grandfather, Rabbi Israel Dayan, came to visit his grandson, who would be the first in the family to make a journey to the Holy Land. The old man and the boy spent much time together. Rubin still had some tubes of oil paint which a friend in Galatz had given him. He had neither canvas nor brushes, so he set to work painting a portrait of his grandfather on cardboard with his fingers (1910; plate 15). He says he can still savor the excitement of the likeness emerging under his hand, and he still keeps the painting with him. The colors have become somewhat dimmed with time, but it is an expressive portrait and a remarkably free and "painterly" effort for an untaught youth of seventeen who had never seen an original painting.

When Rubin arrived in Jerusalem in 1912, it was a sleepy, Oriental city belonging to a province of Turkey. The entire population numbered about sixty thousand, and it is doubtful that anything of artistic value had been created there for hundreds of years. The Bezalel School, housed in a building that had belonged to a French religious order, was a school of crafts rather than of art. There were no art classes to speak of, and the school specialized in turning out objects for the tourist trade. Professor Schatz, on whose help and advice the boy had relied, was away in America. Rubin was without funds and was glad to be taken on to carve decorations on gift boxes of ivory and wood, but he was bitterly disappointed. He had come to study art and not to earn a living decorating souvenirs. The country itself, however, fascinated him from the outset. It was still the land of the Bible, with cities bearing the same names as in the time of Abraham and David and with the same mountains and valleys. He spent all the time he could exploring Jerusalem and its surroundings, and, never without his sketchbook in hand, he made hundreds of drawings. It was during this period he started to sign his work "Reuven" in Hebrew and "Rubin" in English.

One day there occurred one of the chance encounters that have played such a fateful role in Rubin's life. A German tourist who had bought one of the ivory boxes carved by Rubin casually asked him why such a talented youth was wasting his time in a workshop; he should go to Paris, the center of the art world. The idea of studying in Paris had never entered Rubin's mind, but once the suggestion was made, the thought obsessed him. Palestine was still his ultimate goal, but studying in Jerusalem had proved a disappointment. He determined to go to Paris. He sold his few possessions so that he could return to Rumania and there obtain the funds to take him to France.

The journey to his home in Falticeni was full of mishaps, but, as so often with Rubin, good luck helped him in his worst moments. Cholera broke out on the ship, and at Port Said the passengers were put into quarantine. With the exception of Rubin, they were finally allowed to continue on their way, but since he was penniless he was sent under guard to Alexandria. From the prison courtyard he managed to attract the attention of a passerby, who gained Rubin's release by telling the authorities that the young man was a relative for whom he was responsible. Rubin managed to earn some money by making sketches of people in the café near the cheap hotel in which he lodged. His luck did not end there, for chance brought him in contact with an old school friend whose uncle was a director of the Rumanian shipping line in Alexandria. The friend was returning to Rumania and arranged for Rubin to share his cabin.

In Falticeni the situation was unchanged. His family was in its usual state of penury, and shortly after his arrival Rubin looked for work. First he took a job as a bookkeeper in a porcelain factory in the town of Craiova, then he went into business as a grain merchant. At the start he was successful and was able not only to help his family but to put money aside for the projected journey to Paris. Later business took a turn for the worse and he lost most of the money he had made. A relative who believed in his talent managed to obtain a small scholarship of forty-three francs a month for him for a short period from the B'nai B'rith organization, a Jewish philanthropic society, and once this was assured, he made arrangements to leave.

> Paris, city of the arts, what privations I
> suffered within your walls, my beautiful
> City of Lights.[2]

THE PARIS where Rubin arrived in 1913 was a city in the throes of experimentation in art. Pictorial values were being reexamined, and never had the art world been more full of controversy. The first Cubist exhibition had been held in 1911; Picasso was overthrowing accepted notions of what was permissible in painting; Matisse was making bold experiments with color. Jewish artists such as Modigliani and Pascin had become part of the revolutionary art scene. Such sons of the ghetto as Soutine and Pinhas Kremegne arrived in the same year as Rubin; Chagall and Kisling had come three years earlier. But the young man from the Jewish quarter of Galatz, now already twenty, knew nothing of all this. He was still raw, shy, and unworldly, having only his native wits to guide him, but he was filled with a passionate will to be an artist. He knew nobody in Paris and was so naive that he approached no one more competent than the concierge of his little hotel to ask to which art school he should apply. Eventually he made his way to the École des Beaux-Arts, the name of which he had found in a directory of the city's addresses.

Rubin must be considered self-taught. From Professor Colin, who had accepted him as a pupil *hors concours* after seeing his drawings, he received no instruction and actually saw his professor only once during his seven months at the Beaux-Arts. But on that one occasion Professor Colin was sufficiently impressed by Rubin's drawings from the antique to recommend him as a candidate from his atelier for the Prix de Rome. If Rubin had teachers, they were the old masters whom he discovered at the Louvre. He says that he can still remember the intense excitement and the feeling of revelation that possessed him when, for the first time, he saw the paintings of Leonardo and Rembrandt and the frescoes of Fra Angelico, although at the time he did not understand what constituted their greatness. He knew only that the gates of a new world had opened to him.

The months in Paris were heartbreakingly lonely and dogged by poverty. B'nai B'rith stopped sending its small subsidy after one month and had Rubin not been able to enlist the sympathy of Prince Lahovari, the Rumanian ambassador to France who arranged for him to receive a loan, he would have been destitute. There were days when no food passed his lips and he was thankful when a fellow student introduced him to a restaurant in the Rue Tiquetonne where he could get one free meal a day.

His days were spent drawing from plaster casts in the Michelangelo Gallery at the Beaux-Arts (Rue Bonaparte) and in haunting the museums. His free time he passed wandering through the streets, along the banks of the Seine or through the Paris parks. Worse than the penury was the loneliness. He had no one with whom to exchange impressions. He says he looked with envy at the courting couples and the thronged thoroughfares, where everyone except himself seemed to have a companion. As for the cafés of Montparnasse and Montmartre where the artists met, he had no money for such distractions and felt he dared not venture out of his own solitary world. Thus, he had no knowledge of the revolutionary concepts growing up around him.

Inspired by Professor Colin's recommendation that he compete for the prestigious Prix de Rome, Rubin started to teach himself to paint. Although there is still in existence a small canvas of Tel Aviv from 1912 (plate 85)—a simple painting in flat colors of cubelike houses by the seashore, which has a naive charm and shows a certain feeling for composition—Rubin had rarely used oils and had received no training in oil painting. He now decided to study minutely the paintings of Delacroix, whose manipulation of a rich palette had particularly attracted him, and the self-portrait he eventually produced was accepted for exhibition by the Société Nationale des Beaux-Arts. The painting was hung high on the wall in a dark corner and, according to the artist, nobody noticed it except himself and the concierge of his hotel, who was an admirer of his and was able, occasionally, to dispose of his sketches to people in the quarter. It could not have gone entirely unremarked, for he later received some commissions for portrait sketches, which brought him a little badly needed money. This particular portrait has disappeared, but a self-portrait of 1915 clearly shows the influence of Delacroix, with its warm coloring, lively brush strokes, and firmly drawn, well-modeled head (plate 17).

The Beaux-Arts course finished in June, and Rubin then enrolled in the private Académie Colarossi and sketched at the Grande Chaumière atelier in Montparnasse, where there were live models. He began to feel less of a lost soul. "I let my hair grow long and walked through the streets with more assurance." He had his first glimpse of modern daring in the use of color when he saw the works of Matisse at a private gallery, and was "shocked and yet exhilarated." On a visit to Meudon he was introduced to Rodin, and still remembers how much he was impressed by the clasp of the sculptor's large, heavy hand.

17 SELF-PORTRAIT. 1915.
Oil on canvas, 21 × 21".
Collection Mr. and Mrs. David Rubin, Tel Aviv

Rubin never returned to the Beaux-Arts, nor did he have an opportunity to prepare a painting for the Prix de Rome. The First World War broke out at the beginning of August, 1914, and, as a foreigner, he had to leave Paris. His exotic appearance—his mop of black hair, sharp, aquiline features, and long, thin body—aroused suspicion, and it was unpleasant to walk in the streets. Once again friends came to his aid, and at the end of September he was able to leave France for Rumania and home, making the sea voyage by coal freighter.

Nothing was changed in the little town of Falticeni, and Rubin took up his old existence where he had left off, submerged in the familiar feelings of hopelessness and despair. "Only three years before I had leaped into the unknown with my journey to Palestine and later to Paris. And here I was, back where I had started, a prisoner of a war that I felt had nothing to do with me and was slowly draining away my youth."[3]

His sketchbook was a consolation, and he drew constantly the people and the scenes around him. For a glass of brandy he could get the town chimney sweep or the gypsy guitar player to sit for him and could make elaborate, accurate portraits. But there were times when he felt he should abandon all ideas of becoming a painter, since such hopes had no possibility of fulfillment, and then he would pour out his feelings in poetry, turning to Yiddish, the language of his childhood. He had no thought of publication, but putting his feelings into verse brought him some release from emotional tension.

There are nights
Cold, early winter nights
When the pallid moon
Takes pity on the streets
Gazes down with ailing, failing grace
Upon bare trees, and damp roofs
Gazing chill as stone

On nights like these
When curling mist
Twines its veil all over town
Houses look like poor, unhappy

Tattered beggars
Huddled together as though
Telling one another secrets.

On nights like these
Stillness sounds like death.
I alone am living
Long to hold arms over
The world like a cover,
And hug and press it to me.
Will the love within my heart
Be a rising sun
Waking the world to a new dawn?

A number of Jewish intellectuals who had escaped from Russia and Bessarabia had found refuge in Falticeni, and it was to this group that Rubin gravitated, and whose talk and sympathy saved him from utter despondency. But sketches and poetry did not help solve the family's perennial money troubles, and before long Rubin took a job in a leather factory that belonged to one of his uncles. He acted as accountant, humdrum work that he disliked and that he made a little more palatable by using the margins of the account books to make drawings and caricatures of the customers. The uncle went on a purchasing trip to Italy, taking Rubin with him as his assistant. The young man soon became bored with all the business details, and, when his relative returned to Rumania, leaving Rubin to complete arrangements, he seized the opportunity to visit the museums and galleries of Rome and Florence. He recalls particularly the tremendous impression made on him by the monumentality of the figures and the grandeur of design in the works of Giotto and Piero della Francesca. In Rome he was able to sell some caricatures to newspapers, but one such drawing, lampooning Hindenburg, was considered to have passed permissible bounds, and the police ordered him to leave the country. He went to Switzerland, and it was in Zurich that he saw the exhibition by the now more-or-less forgotten modernist Ferdinand Hodler that was to have considerable influence on his early work. It was not only the bold simplification of Hodler's composition and the religious and national symbolism of his conceptions that struck a responsive

chord in the young Rubin but also a personal contact with the artist. For the first
time he had occasion to meet and talk with an eminent painter who could expound
to him something of his aesthetic philosophy, and he was deeply affected by this.

Rubin had no legal right of residence in Switzerland, neither had he the funds
with which to support himself, and at the same time his employer was urgently
demanding his return to Falticeni. So, some six weeks after his departure, he was
back at his old job in the leather factory. Again depression enveloped him. He tried
his hand at sculpture but with little success; he soon abandoned his fumbling at-
tempts and turned once again to poetry.

NIGHT

Earth is a corpse
A carcass, black and
Wrapped in shadows of the night.
Heavens drop pearls
And tears.
Stars—
Soul-lights at the corpse's head.

Book open wide.
Old man turning
Page after page.
The holy chants of
Words on words
Drop without start or stop.

Cottage pulls
Roof down on brow
Trembles, puts out
Light in eye.
Blind, alone
Like a night watchman
Cottage stands
Shoulders bent and stains the night.

18 Rubin in Bucharest, 1917

He began to read voraciously, mainly the philosophers Schopenhauer, Nietzsche, and Carlyle and the Russian novelists Tolstoi, Dostoevski, Gogol, and Turgenev. Rubin has a natural gift for languages and today is fluent in a half-dozen, but, at the time, he read the books in the original languages with the help of dictionaries. Soon he had little opportunity for reading or writing poetry, however. Rumania entered the war in the summer of 1916; the leather factory started to work for the war effort, and Rubin was fully occupied. Food became scarce and people died of hunger. Typhus epidemics broke out, claiming the members of his family one by one, and medical care was almost unobtainable.

When the war was over Rubin went back to Galatz for a while, and then left for Bucharest. It had been badly damaged during the war and many of the buildings were completely destroyed, but he was able to find a small room. An acquaintance allowed him to have the use of an old bathroom, and, with running water at hand, he was able to continue his experiments with sculpture. He started by modeling heads; these were crude, but seemed to show that he had a certain aptitude. He then taught himself how to make an armature out of bits of wood and wire, and eventually he modeled the figure of a man praying, which was cast in plaster but has since disappeared. To earn a living he designed furniture and ornamental objects in wood and clay. A short visit to Falticeni was followed by a return to Bucharest, where by then he had a circle of friends, mainly Jewish writers and musicians. He worked at both painting and sculpture but without material success. He tried his hand at various jobs, even, at the suggestion of relatives, becoming a jam manufacturer for a short while. At the beginning of 1919, after much disappointment and mental suffering, he left for Czernowitz, the capital of Bukovina, which had been annexed to Rumania from the Ukraine. It was reputedly the Rumanian Vienna, and Rubin believed he would find its atmosphere congenial and at last be able to devote himself to painting. He was now twenty-six and was driven by the feeling that his life was slipping past without his having even started to accomplish what he most desired. Soon after his arrival he met Arthur Kolnik, a painter a few years older than he, who had been born in the small town of Stanislav, then in eastern Austria (now USSR), had studied at the Cracow Academy of Art, and had settled in Czernowitz a year previously. They became friends and Kolnik gave Rubin his first lessons in the technique of oil painting. The two young artists worked together, leading for the most part what Rubin later described as "a hermit existence, seeking to heal in ourselves the wounds inflicted by war."[4]

It was during the eighteen months he spent in Czernowitz that Rubin executed the paintings and sculpture that were to be exhibited in New York in 1921. A self-portrait cast in bronze, one of the few early pieces that can still be traced, shows the Rubin of 1920 as a tormented creature (plate 19). Misery and discontent are marked on every feature of the face, which is modeled in a manner combining the realistic with the romantic. Clearly he had a natural talent for sculpture, which, however, he gave up to devote himself entirely to painting. The furrowed brow of his self-portrait, the narrowed eyes with deep pouches under them, and the protruding underlip all speak of the unhappiness and revolt that possessed him at the time. It was during this mood of depression and pessimism that he painted canvases with such names as *Meal of the Poor, Madonna of the Homeless,* and *Temptation in the Desert,* which were shown at his first exhibition in New York in 1921.

Such friends as Rubin made were drawn from the Jewish intellectuals in the city; these included the fabulist Eliezer Steinberg, the poet Itzhak Manger, the novelist Moshe Altman, and the essayist Shlomo Bickel, all of whom wrote in Yiddish. In this society Rubin was again encouraged to turn to writing poetry when the urge to paint or sculpt left him for a while. Little by little he was able to sell an occasional painting or piece of sculpture and gradually he felt more at home in Czernowitz than he had felt anywhere else. Restless by nature, however, and always conscious that the world was wide, he began to think of moving. A visitor to his studio talked of the United States and the infinite opportunities offered by that vast and vital country, and Rubin became fired by the notion of going to New York and exhibiting there. But he did not have the means to travel, and so he decided to go to Bucharest to enlist the help of people he knew. He knocked at many doors in vain until his closest friend, Bernard Weinberg, a lover of music and art and then secretary of the Zionist organization in the city (today he lives in the south of France and owns the largest collection of Rubin's early works), suggested he introduce Rubin to his employer, Lazar Margulies, then an important figure in Rumanian finance. Margulies was sufficiently impressed by the young painter to lend him the sum necessary to take him and Arthur Kolnik to New York.

RUBIN has often said that at first New York, with its forest of tall buildings and hurrying crowds, inspired in him a feeling of dread. He felt lost, bewildered, and of no account, and wondered how he had dared venture into such a metropolis. The first months were wretched. He had no connections at all with the New York art world, and the only people he knew were a brother of his father's who lived on the Lower East Side, and the director of the Rumanian bank to which his paintings had been consigned. He lost the urge to paint and spent most of his time walking about New York with Kolnik. By chance, he made the acquaintance of some Jewish writers, with whom he became friendly and with whom he rented at small cost an old shabby house in Far Rockaway, where he passed the summer months in pleasant company. With the approach of autumn he returned to New York, physically refreshed but low in spirits. He had been some six months in America and had not been able even to take the first steps toward arranging an exhibition. As he recalls it, "I was haunted by a feeling of time wasted and was afraid I would sink into a state of apathy, when I would not be able to grasp an opportunity even if it were offered to me." But shortly Rubin was to meet a man who would not only help establish him as a professional painter but would also confirm his belief in himself as an artist. This was Alfred Stieglitz, the noted photographer and art patron, who had a remarkable flair for recognizing new talent. Stieglitz found impressive qualities in Rubin's paintings, with the result that an exhibition was arranged for November in the then well-known Anderson Gallery.

The exhibition by two unknown painters from faraway Rumania aroused interest in the New York art world, which at the time was excited by the first big show of Impressionist and Post-Impressionist paintings, and the *New York World* wrote: "In view of the present controversy over the modernistic paintings shown at the Metropolitan Museum of Art, the offerings at the Anderson Gallery are doubly interesting,"[5] while the *New York American* stated: "Think of two such apocalyptic artists opening a show in materialistic New York with the idea of 'possibly selling some of their pictures.' It is preposterous and yet it is sublime. The very audacity of faith and despair may triumph at that."[6]

Of Rubin *The New York Times* wrote: "The self he expresses is ardent and very young. He knows his craft. In spite of the dreary subjects, the gallery vibrates with light, strong colors laid on with simplicity and directness."[7] The painter himself was described by Louis Bernheimer in the *Sunday World* as "toreadoresque; [he] wears sideburns down his hollow cheeks, has a wave of black hair that breaks to the left, burning black eyes, a small red mouth, looking like one of Zuloaga's bullfighters." To that writer Rubin said: "My forebears are Gauguin, Van Gogh, Cézanne, and Hodler. I am not at all interested in copying nature. I only wish to express the idea of a supreme being. I am a seeker of God, a god who will end the suffering of humanity. I seek him in line, colour, and movement."[8]

Of the works shown at this exhibition, it has been possible to trace four, three of which are in private collections in Tel Aviv: *Meal of the Poor, Encounter,* and *Temptation in the Desert* (1920; plate 20). The fourth, *False Prophets* (1920; plate 99), belongs to a London gallery. The painter has no knowledge of the whereabouts of the others. A few were sold at the time, and "others were given to someone whose name I no longer recall as payment for debts."

The New York Times referred to the fact that these paintings made no attempt to please, and it is clear that Rubin was struggling to express his emotional disturbances and his dissatisfaction with life rather than to create decorative compositions. It is not difficult to understand that, like other young painters of that time with similar problems, he found his master in the Swiss symbolist Hodler. *Temptation in the Desert,* for example, shows three figures stretched out in a sandy waste, with a crouching woman trying to clutch the robes of an emaciated figure standing in the center. The colors are the pale ochers and grays of the desert; on one ridge appear cactus shrubs, a reminder of Rubin's year in Palestine. The drawing is strong, with heavy contour lines, and the large bony hands are emphasized, in the manner of Hodler. The symbolism is both personal and general; Rubin describes the central figure as himself resisting worldly temptation personified by the woman. The face of the standing man is that of his brother, killed in the First World War.

These works are unique in Rubin's *oeuvre*. There is no hint in them of the paintings he was later to produce and never again did he return to these tragic themes.

It was with relief that Rubin left New York to go back to Rumania. In spite of his success—for such it could be termed in the circumstances—his stay gave him no satisfaction except for his friendship with Stieglitz. As a parting gift his sponsor gave him a copy of Marsden Hartley's *Adventures in Art,* writing in the inscription "I wish

19 SELF-PORTRAIT. 1920.
Bronze, height 18".
Collection Mr. and Mrs. B. Weinberg, Paris

20 TEMPTATION IN THE DESERT. 1920. Oil on canvas, 38 × 52″.
Ida Kimche Gallery, Tel Aviv

you only *Ausdauer* [persistence], the rest you have." These words have remained a source of encouragement and comfort to the artist.

On the way home Rubin stopped briefly in Paris and Vienna and then stayed a short time with his family in Falticeni before moving on to Bucharest. There he rented an empty garage, which he turned into a studio, and started to give his time again to painting. Always a rapid worker, he completed in a short while a sufficient number of canvases for an exhibition, which was held in his own studio. One of the paintings from this period that Rubin still possesses, *Procession with Torah* (1921; plate 88), with its elimination of detail, simple monumentality of the two central figures, clear, pale color, and somewhat naive design, presages the works he was to execute in the following years in Palestine. Against the background of the academic nineteenth-century painting then prevalent in Rumania, Rubin's work appeared "revolutionary," and it is not surprising that reviewers so hailed it.

A return to Palestine was always in Rubin's mind, and when an opportunity arose to act as leader of a group of immigrants leaving for that country, he seized it immediately.

HE ARRIVED at the port of Jaffa in the early autumn of 1922 and at once set off for Jerusalem. There he found that the sleepy, almost medieval Turkish backwater which he had left ten years previously was moving into the twentieth century and starting to become a modern city. It was the seat of the British mandatory administration. Roads and new buildings were being constructed, and among the rising Jewish population were many intellectuals and a number of artists. Rubin struck up a close friendship with the sculptor Aaron Melnikov, who had settled in Jerusalem in 1918 and whose studio on the Old Wall over the Damascus Gate had become a center of the artistic life of the city.

Rubin says that from the start he felt he had "come home," that the light was his light and this was the air he could most easily breathe. He had no sooner settled into the room he had rented with a Bokharian family than he started to work, and it is from his first weeks in Jerusalem that his *Girl with Pomegranates* (plate 21) and *Donkey Rider* (plate 22) date. The painter was fascinated by the dark beauty of many of the Oriental girls, and the girl in the canvas, who stares out with her huge Byzantine eyes, her pose hieratic, a plait of long black hair over her shoulder, with one hand holding a dish of pomegranates in the forefront of the painting, was the first of several such figures he was to paint over the next years. Already to be noted is the way in which Rubin composes the background from elements of landscape arranged in a formal pattern, which became a characteristic of his early work. The color scheme, predominantly cold blues and pale pinky-oranges, indicates a natural skill in the balancing of color harmonies. In the *Donkey Rider* we find a motif that was to become a favorite with the painter: an Arab boy astride a donkey, playing a flute. In certain paintings the flute would be replaced by a bouquet of flowers. Again the figure is framed by a landscape pattern, while the strong curve of the animal's neck and head dominates the foreground, and in the background a small figure is introduced to provide an accent and to give scale. It is the type of curvilinear composition that Rubin favors; apparently this is a natural predilection, for it is seldom that he employs angular forms or straight lines.

After some months in Jerusalem, Rubin moved to Tel Aviv, which then had a population of over 15,000 and which was attracting younger artists, who saw in the city a symbol of the pioneering life of the country and themselves as the initiators of a new Israeli art. Rubin was taken by the spirit of youthful and constructive enthusiasm in the city, and with his love for the blue expanse of the sea, he set up house in a tent on the dunes by the seashore. As he recalls it, he spent hours looking at the small fishing boats floating on the waves, at the caravans of camels with their native drivers, making their way over the sands, and at the herds of goats that fed on the meager shrubs near his tent. All this was to find expression in his paintings.

After a short while he moved into an old house on the Jaffa border, and it was then he wrote: "A new life springs up around me. I feel the sap of creative energy rising in me too. I have thrown away all the ideas I had derived from the Bezalel Art School and the Paris Beaux-Arts. The world is clear and pure to me. Life is stark, bare, primitive. I do not feel burdened by problems and I find it easy to work." Less than a year after his return to Palestine, he held his first one-man show in the country. Since at the time there were no museums or art galleries, exhibitions were held in schools, private homes, or clubs. Rubin's exhibition took place at the Herzlia High School, the largest building in Tel Aviv. A friend recalls that "in those days the opening of an art exhibition was an event which attracted all sections of the

21 GIRL WITH POMEGRANATES.
1922. Oil on canvas,
33 × 29 ¼″. Collection
Charles Clore, London

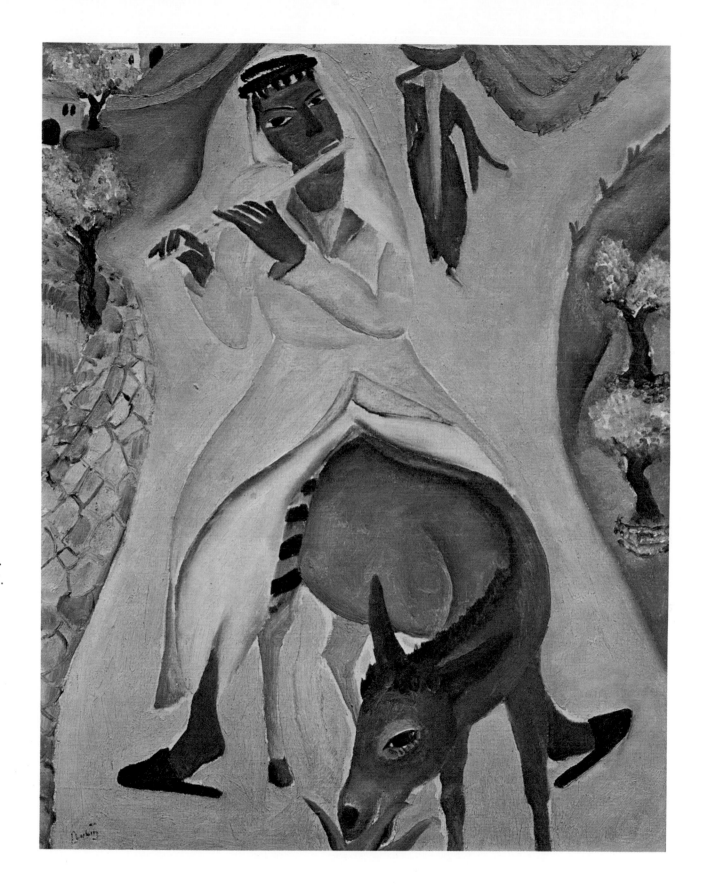

22 DONKEY RIDER. 1922.
Oil on canvas, 26 × 20″.
Collection Mr. and
Mrs. B. Weinberg, Paris

community who came to see the paintings out of curiosity if for no other reason. The Rubin show occasioned real excitement and enthusiasm among artlovers and was a subject for discussion at the cafés, which were the usual meeting places." A writer in the Hebrew daily *Doar Hayom* summed up the general feeling: "There is no doubt that Rubin is a pure artist. Simple lines, clear colors, distinct forms, . . . understanding of the truth, a love of the world and its longings."[9] Rubin turned to the life around him for his subjects, viewing them with the fresh and innocent eye of a man who had fallen in love with the new world he had entered, and finding a fitting simplicity and directness with which to express his delight. *Succoth in Jerusalem* (1925; plate 111), *Flowers in My Window* (now in the Tel Aviv Museum), *First Fruits,* and *Yemenite Family* were the titles of some of the paintings. Writing some thirty years later, the late Dr. E. Kolb, then director of the Tel Aviv Museum, said of *First Fruits* (1923; plate 92), that it "represents a document of that epoch when pioneers brought forth the first fruits of the soil of this ancient land. Rubin's youth was the youth of Eretz Israel and his work conjures up wistful recollections of that happy and courageous time."[10]

In general, the works of the small group of artists then in Palestine bear a family resemblance, but from the outset Rubin showed an individuality of his own. The paintings of the period that have remained in the collection of the artist and of the Tel Aviv Museum are marked by directness and integrity. Composition is simple and colors are sun-bleached and flatly applied. Black contour lines and accents sharply contrast with the dominant pale pinks, ochers, and blues. These canvases reveal the love and understanding with which he approached his subjects; with amazing quickness he captured the essential qualities and the pictorial possibilities of this new-old country and its people.

Fifty years of prolific work were to follow his initial experiments.

In 1923 Rubin produced an album of twelve woodcuts, *The God Seekers* (plates 23–25), undertaking the actual printing himself since there was nobody else competent to do it. More than forty years later, these same woodcuts were republished in a limited edition (sixty sets) by the Bineth Gallery of Jerusalem, with a foreword by Dr. Haim Gamzu, the present director of the Tel Aviv Museum. He finds that the woodcuts are "charged with the atmosphere of prayer" and that the strong contrasts between black and white, light and dark, refer to the "collision between two worlds, that of the traditional life and faith of the Jewish town in the Diaspora and that of the new ideal of the Jew replanted in his own homeland." Thus an important work of Rubin's youth finally found its way to the public.

Many of the themes of these woodcuts were later to reappear in paintings; *Immigrants at Rest,* for example, which depicts a man, woman, and child resting by the roadside, would be transformed, with certain changes, into Rubin's several versions of *Rest on the Flight.*

At the beginning of 1924, Rubin approached Sir Ronald Storrs, then governor of Jerusalem and a man keenly interested in art and music, who had become his personal friend, with the request that he be allowed to use the massive Jerusalem Citadel, known as the Tower of David, for an exhibition. Constructed in the time of Herod and unused for centuries, the building was encased in grime and filled with rubbish, but a magnificent, hexagonal inner hall was discovered, well lighted from above. Friends were enlisted to put the place in order, and a line of white-painted cans containing shrubs was laid down, leading from the Jaffa Gate of the Old City to the entrance. Posters and invitations were printed in the three official languages— English, Hebrew, and Arabic. Everybody taking part was filled with enthusiasm, and the opening, in the first week of March, aroused considerable excitement. Rubin was feted as the first artist to hold an exhibition in the Citadel. "The exhibition was a pleasant surprise to the Jerusalem public, which had never before witnessed anything approaching this new trend of creative art. Every painting displays the individuality of the artist, powerful design, and vivid coloring, and places Rubin in a class by himself," wrote the *Palestine Weekly*.[11] The Tower of David was later to house annual exhibitions of the newly formed Association of Palestine Artists, which comprised the more "advanced" artists of the time and of which Rubin was an initiator.

The exhibition attracted the attention of all sections of the population of Jerusalem and its vicinity, and the *Haaretz,* the leading Hebrew daily, wrote: "It was interesting to see a group of five orthodox Jews, with beards and side curls, from the Old City coming to the Rubin exhibition yesterday. Unfortunately they did not have enough money to buy tickets for all of them (five piasters each). So they cast lots and the winner collected a piaster from each and then entered the Tower of David to see the show."[12]

23–25 DANCERS AT MERON; WATER CARRIER; SELF-PORTRAIT. 1923.
Three woodcuts from the album *The God Seekers*. Each 33 × 28″

It was here that Rubin exhibited his first Jerusalem townscapes, with the walled city and the Mosque of Omar and its dome dominating the composition and with the mountain background, dotted with cypresses and cut by winding paths. Painted two-dimensionally in flat, rich earth colors, with map-like contour lines and sharply defined detail, they depict a medieval city, sunk in time, and in their design are reminiscent of Persian miniatures; yet already they bear the impress of Rubin's personal pictorial feeling.

These early primitive paintings have often been likened to the works of the Douanier Rousseau, although Rubin emphatically denies having seen any of that artist's work at that time. That there is a resemblance cannot be gainsaid, and perhaps it is

26 Rubin with a group of artist friends
at his first exhibition
at the Tower of David, Jerusalem, 1924

due to the feeling for bold simplification and for decorative composition that is characteristic of both. Or maybe, as Eric Newton has stated: "The artist who falls in love with each separate object and intensifies each separate color is bound to remind one of Rousseau. . . . What accounts for a superficial similarity of style is the quality of their intense affection."[13]

In the recollection of his friends, Rubin at the time painted in an "intoxication of creativity." He seemed to work without pause, and apparently without effort. He traveled through Galilee, stopping at Tiberias on the Lake of Kinneret and the terrace-town of Safed, home of the Cabala, taking the road to Meron and finding everywhere subjects for his brush. One friend remembers that Rubin walked through the streets of Tel Aviv, swinging a cane and always with a flower in the lapel of his jacket, clearly a man at peace with the world. Another friend says that what distinguished Rubin's work from that of other painters who were similarly responding to the spiritual and physical climate of their new homeland was "the emotion of happy love that emanated from his canvases. He was a man deeply in love with his country and able to convey this feeling to the viewer."

The dream of every artist, an exhibition in Paris, now gripped the painter. He had already held two exhibitions in Palestine and had accumulated a large number of canvases which he was anxious to show to a more understanding public; he also wished to receive informed criticism. He borrowed the additional money he needed for his journey from friends, and, since his circle in Bucharest insisted he exhibit there the works painted in Palestine, he went first to Rumania. The exhibition brought favorable reviews, most of them expressing astonishment at his new style, but Rubin remembers that financially the exhibition was not very successful. During his stay, however, he designed the decor and costumes for the performance of *The Singer of His Sorrow,* given by the famous group of Yiddish actors who made up the Vilna Troupe, with Joseph Buloff.

Rubin arrived in Paris toward the end of 1924. His position was similar to that of some ten years previously, in that he had no friends in the city and had no contact with its art life. He found a cheap room for himself in a millinery store and again spent most of his time visiting museums and galleries. By chance he met the sculptress Chana Orloff, well known in Parisian art circles, who originally came from Palestine. She introduced Rubin to the French-Jewish writer and poet Edmond Fleg, and it was at the Fleg home that he met Mme. Bernheim of the well-known art dealer's family. Mme. Bernheim, with some friends, came to see Rubin's paintings, which, as he remembers, he kept under the bed in his room. She was much taken with his work, with the result that he was offered an exhibition, which took place in the spring of 1925. Edmond Fleg wrote an appreciative foreword to the catalogue, in which he spoke of the paintings as "calm and transparent, filled with an iridescent light which seems to ignore the contrast of shadows, intimate serenity of postures and faces, relaxation and repose. All is harmony, harmony."

The tranquil mood of the paintings, their light, joyous colors, and their freedom from the tensions and suffering that were associated with the works of Jewish painters occasioned widely expressed surprise. The response to the exhibition was favorable, and Rubin was offered a five-year contract, with the proviso that he stay in Paris and paint there. But he knew there was only one country where he could express himself, and that was Palestine. French culture attracted him, which made him all the more wary of being submerged by it and losing his individuality. He did spend some more months in Paris, becoming acquainted with the works of such painters as Vlaminck, Derain, and Dufy, whose art he had not known before, and, through his friend Chana Orloff, he met both Pascin and Kisling and visited their studios. But the Bohemian lives they led held no appeal for him, and he was not excited by the ferment of experimentation in the French capital. He instinctively realized that his path lay elsewhere, and he was happy to return to Tel Aviv.

> Here in Jerusalem, Tel Aviv, Haifa, and Tiberias I feel myself reborn. Only here do I feel that life and nature are mine. The grey clouds of Europe have disappeared. . . . All is sunshine, clear light, and happy, creative work. As the desert revives and blooms under the hands of the pioneers, so do I feel awakening in me all the latent energies. . . . I live with simple people, I walk the old Galilean roads and ride on horseback from Ir Ganim to Tel Aviv with milkmen and farmers. The horizon has broad, curved lines. The air is clear and transparent, and the perspective of European atmosphere no longer deforms nature for me. Men here are simple dreamers. Life is full of surprises for them. Everything is new, and their wide-open eyes regard the world with wonderment. I have pitched my tent on these ancient hills, and my desire is to tie together the ends of the thread that history has broken.[14]

BY NOW Rubin felt himself sufficiently rooted in his new country to bring over from Rumania his mother and sister and to rent an apartment in one of the new houses that had been built facing the Mediterranean. He was able to do this with the proceeds from his Paris exhibition. His much-loved father died before he could make the journey.

At this time he designed the costumes and decor for Richard Ber Hoffmann's *Jacob's Dream* for the newly formed Hatai, the theatrical company headed by Menahem Gnessin with the young actor Finkel (now the art director of the Habimah Theatre) in the lead.

The next couple of years were a period of intense activity—a period of splendid creativity when some of his most important canvases were painted. Undoubtedly the dynamic art life of Paris, although he had savored it only for a few months, had made considerable impact and given an added strength to his work. To these years belong the big canvases of *My Family, Dancers of Meron* (1926; plate 29), and *Jews of Jerusalem*.

The family portrait (1925; plate 28) was one of the first pictures painted after his return from Paris. The mother, dressed in black relieved with white at throat and wrist, her hands crossed on her lap, is the central focus. To her left sits the painter himself, brush in one hand, palette in the other, with red slippers on his feet. Behind the mother are Rubin's brother and sister; she holds a flower in her hand, providing a touch of more resonant color against the pale pink of her dress. At the right is a black goat, linked to the group by that "feeling of tenderness and familiarity between man and animal" on which the French art critic Florent Fels has commented. The figures, posed as if for an old-fashioned photograph, and depicted with a primitive rigidity, are set against a background of silvery olive grove, and not an inch of canvas is left unexploited. Characteristically for Rubin, at this time as well as later, the faces are without modeling; they are schematized, with emphasis given to the eyes. In its harmony of color, directness of execution, and simplicity of well-balanced design, the painting is among the best and most typical of the artist's work at the time. It was shown at the exhibition of the Palestine Artists Association held at the Jerusalem Citadel in 1926 and was awarded the Lord Plumer Prize. It now belongs to the Tel Aviv Museum.

In the following year, 1927, Rubin held his second exhibition in Tel Aviv. The great Hebrew poet Chaim Nachman Bialik wrote the catalogue introduction, which even today remains one of the most penetrating analyses of the sources of Rubin's work and of what he sought to accomplish. With the intuitive understanding of the creator, Bialik wrote:

This land of Israel that is presented to us in Rubin's paintings, as he sees it, whole and entire, with its mountains and towns, its gardens and valleys, its old men and women, its Arabs and Jews, its donkeys and goats, its stones and plants, with all

27 Portrait of Rubin in bronze by Chana Orloff, 1925

50

28 MY FAMILY. 1925.
Oil on canvas, 64 × 50 ½".
Tel Aviv Museum (Lord Plumer Prize)

these, as a rule, brought together and assorted in unexpected association on one small canvas—this land of Israel appears to us like a Midrashic legend, the legend of Eretz Israel. [The Midrash is the book of the Jewish sages explicating the Bible, mainly through allegorical stories.] It was thus that this land appeared to us and was imprinted on our imagination and our mind in our childhood, . . . and it was thus that we have borne and cherished it in our hearts. . . . This is how things are seen by a child, by popular legend, and by the artist. Whoever wishes to see the land of Israel and all that is connected with it in its transcendent purity should turn to the paintings of Rubin.

Writing of Rubin's work during the twenties, Yona Fischer, curator of the contemporary art section of the Israel Museum in Jerusalem, said: ''His portrait of the sculptor Melnikov against a background of houses [now in the Tel Aviv Museum] and his Jaffa landscapes seen through an open window, point to the expressive qualities of Rubin's early work in Israel. His style, romantic yet extremely simple, is characterized by its complete adaptation to a new visual world.''[15]

As the English art critic Eric Newton has pointed out, Rubin is possessed by ''strong feeling for the human activity that springs from the soil,''[16] and, from the early days of his settlement in Palestine, shepherds tending their sheep, the Arab fellahin at work threshing or picking olives, and fishermen casting their nets or sorting their catch were subjects of innumerable drawings. But it was not until the late twenties that he began to be occupied with the fisherman as a motif for painting, a motif that was to recur in his canvases. Among the most successful is the *Jaffa Fisherman Family* (1927; plate 124). The stalwart figure of the fisherman displaying his catch dominates the carefully built-up composition, of which the strong verticals are unusual for Rubin. At his side are wife and child, a trio of figures set against a bright blue sea on which a sailboat rides. All is harmonious and calm. While the faces and hands are painted in broad, flat colors, the pigment is applied to the clothes, fish, basket, and even to the background in such a way as to draw attention to their different tactile qualities. It appears that the artist's interest in surface textures dates from this year. The entire color scheme, enlivened by small, broken touches of the brush, is more varied than previously, and it is clear that his stay in Paris influenced his handling of paint, although his artistic vision remained personal, as it has throughout his painting career.

At the beginning of 1928 Rubin again became restless, and, having accumulated a large collection of canvases, set off for Paris. There was little difficulty in arranging an exhibition, which took place at the Druet Gallery. Critical response was warm, and, in an article in *Chroniques et Documents*, art critic Jean Topaz wrote of "a new Hebrew primitivism with Hebraic sources, authentically of this holy, promised land—promised and refound. . . ." He said further:

> He is the painter *instinctif*, who has discovered the joy of living and painting. In the canvas *Dancers of Meron* [plate 29] the general arabesque is perfectly enclosed, conclusive, definite; and the elements which compose the painting are combined with force and correctness: the group of dancers who form a block, the bouquet of women (à la Fra Angelico) who flank the right, the grey ribbon of road that winds, sometimes narrow, sometimes wide, carrying a small figure on a donkey, the balance of the hills that cross the entire picture. If one can say of a single person that he founded a school then I would say that with Rubin, the "Palestine style" has been born.[17]

Although from the point of view of critical reception the exhibition was a success, and a landscape, *Village of Sumeil*, was purchased by the French government, there was little material gain, and the artist was perplexed as to what his next move should be. The director of the well-known gallery Arthur Tooth and Sons in London had visited the exhibition and been impressed, and Rubin went over to London for a brief stay, during which an exhibition at the Tooth Gallery was arranged for 1930. He considered the possibility of taking his collection to New York, where, seven years previously, he had shown his very early "apocalyptic" paintings. Since then his work had changed completely, and he felt he had something new and personal to show. But he had not the necessary funds, and a letter of introduction to a gallery director, George S. Hellman, had brought the reply that the latter had given up his gallery. A chance meeting with an American acquaintance resulted in the offer of a loan, and Rubin decided that, prepared or not, he would make the venture. In May he embarked for the U.S.A.

These months in the United States were a happy period in Rubin's life. While the following year was to bring the Wall Street Crash and country-wide depression, in 1928 all seemed optimistic and prosperous. He was no longer the unhappy, apprehensive young man of his first visit. Living in his own homeland had given him confidence. He rented a studio apartment in Manhattan and started to enjoy what the big city had to offer. As summer approached he was invited to spend a month with friends at Lake Placid. The trees, the green lawns, and the blue lake enchanted him; it was the first real holiday he had ever had. He began to paint his surroundings, but found that the lush serenity of the landscape, beautiful to the eye as it was, with its predominance of varied greens, did not act as the spur to his imagination he needed for creation, and later he destroyed nearly everything he had painted. In the little granddaughter of his hosts, however, he found a subject close to his heart, and a portrait study of her already shows the tender understanding of childhood that, many years later, he was to express in the portraits of his own children.

It happened that George Hellman was also vacationing in the vicinity. The two men, who knew of one another from correspondence, now met. They immediately established a sympathetic relationship, and Hellman came to see Rubin's paintings in his New York studio. He not only brought the works to the attention of the director of the Guarino Gallery, so that an exhibition was arranged for the beginning of December, but himself wrote the foreword to the catalogue, which he entitled "Palestine's Gauguin." The French painter, he wrote, "became the discoverer of Tahiti, but also of the new Gauguin. In similar fashion, though with deeper spiritual emphasis, Rubin may be regarded as the artistic interpreter of Palestine's new life and landscape as envisioned by a new Rubin."

George Hellman grasped the fundamental fact that it was in Palestine—in the land of the Bible that the artist felt so deeply to be his true homeland—that Rubin was also able to discover himself. As he has so often said, and as circumstances have borne out: in no other country could he feel completely at home or paint with such a feeling of fulfillment.

Writing in the August, 1928, issue of the *Studio* (London), New York critic William Schack spoke of Rubin's "serenity and gusto, two qualities not often found together, [which] characterize his work—serenity and gusto: these pulsate in the major rhythms of his pictures and make vivid the details." And in the December issue of the *Menorah Journal* of that year, the same critic, analyzing Rubin's work up to that time, wrote:

29 DANCERS OF MERON. 1926.
Oil on canvas, 64 × 50 ½".
The Rubin Museum Foundation

Primarily it seems to be an archaic quality that Rubin sees in his subjects and sets down. These fishermen, milkmen, donkey boys, Hassidim—in all of them he finds a remoteness, a dream-like character, as if they existed by themselves between earth and sky, away from all human conflicts. . . . . There is very little groping in Rubin's canvases. Even his most incomplete pictures impress one with their own assurance of wholeness. They seem to be the product of a mind singularly free from inner conflicts, as, in fact, they are. It is a serene nature that expresses itself in these imperturbable, unfaltering pictures.

William Schack misunderstood the painter's nature. Rubin is, and, according to his old friends, always was, an excitable, tense, and easily perturbed man. But when he stands in front of his easel, the stresses and worries of daily life disappear. The very act of applying paint to canvas calms him. He is filled with the joy of creation; ease of spirit pervades his being and expresses itself in the tranquil harmony of his paintings.

Reviews of the exhibition were highly favorable; many collectors bought paintings, and both the Brooklyn and Newark museums acquired works. Rubin was now in a position to fulfill a cherished dream: to buy a plot of land in Palestine and to plant an orange grove.

In the early spring of 1929, he booked passage to Palestine on the *Mauretania,* which was making a Mediterranean cruise, embarking on what he has since called "the most fateful journey of my life." On board ship was a beautiful young American girl, still in her teens. She was Esther Davis of New York, who had won a national oratory contest with a prize of a trip to Palestine. This was the girl destined to be Rubin's wife. Reminiscing, he says that he fell in love with her as soon as she looked at him with her large, sea-colored eyes, but it took a year's pursuit to convince her to link her life with his. Esther was to prove the ideal helpmate, with an intuitive understanding of the demands of the artist's temperament, a finely disciplined intelligence, and outstanding gifts as a hostess. Rubin, conscious since boyhood of an inner loneliness and a feeling of isolation, felt for the first time that another human being was emotionally involved with him in mutual love and sympathy. Maybe it was this close relationship with someone with whom he could share not only his impressions but his inmost thoughts that brought about the new turn in Rubin's development toward the end of the twenties.

Up to that time, the greater part of his work had consisted of figure compositions, very often with highly formal landscape pattern as part of the background. He had painted a few landscapes proper, notably of Jerusalem, Tiberias, and Safed, but these were of a stylized, schematic type, in which the actual facts of the scene were subordinated to his over-all design. Now, traveling around the country with a loved companion who was responsive to scenery new to her, he became conscious of the natural landscape and its trees and flowers in a way he never had before. He has described this new awareness in his autobiographical sketches, *My Life, My Art:*

> I can recall exactly when this happened to me. I was on my way to Jerusalem with Esther on one of our many trips together. We approached the beautiful village of Abu Ghosh, surrounded by ancient olive trees. I stopped the car and stood amazed, for I saw the countryside in a completely different way than I ever had before. It seemed to me that the landscape and its olive trees were leaning towards me, embracing me. The colors, the light, the shimmering atmosphere in which the landscape seemed to breathe and live—it was like a revelation. I took out my sketchbook and started to draw, making notes of colors I had never noticed before. . . .
> In my studio afterwards, I would cover many canvases, attempting to recapture my feeling at the moment when I "discovered" the beauty of the natural landscape.[18]

This "discovery" led Rubin to begin painting the lyrically conceived landscapes with olive trees and cypress-dotted mountain villages that, although not depicting the actualities of any particular place, so compellingly evoke the spirit and atmosphere of Galilee and Judea and that have become almost synonymous with his name as a painter. From the late twenties, his painting shows an added subtlety of color, fuller use of pigment, and livelier brushwork—hence, a greater sense of animation.

He became so fascinated by the olive trees, with their gnarled, twisted, heavy trunks and feathery, silvery-gray leaves, that he painted them again and again under varying atmospheric conditions. In these paintings of the end of the twenties, he tried to put on canvas a faithful description of what his eyes saw, and the English art critic R. H. Wilenski, reviewing Rubin's exhibition in London at the Tooth Gallery in 1930, wrote: "Hundreds of artists have painted olive trees, but I have rarely seen their silver sheen in the sunlight more convincingly rendered."[19]

He was the first, in fact the only, painter in the country at that time to attempt to capture the dazzling native light and to depict the effect created by the khamsin, the hot wind that blows from the desert and puts a haze over everything, appearing to turn the whole world into colored air (plate 44). In general, the Palestinian painters avoided tackling the problems posed by the heat and light. Moreover, many of them had gone to Paris in the middle twenties to seek fresh impetus and to pick up new ideas, for not only were they experiencing a feeling of stultification in their work, now that the first naively romantic reaction to their new homeland was over, but the country was going through an economic depression, during which, as always, artists were among the first to suffer. When they returned, usually after a stay of a year or so, they tended to see the country in terms of the gray skies and green fields of France and to reproduce versions of School of Paris paintings. Rubin too had spent time in Paris, first as a student and again in 1925 and in 1928, in connection with his exhibitions there. He had certainly not been uninfluenced by what he saw of French painting, but his instinct led him to reject what was alien to his purpose, and his passionate love for the Palestine landscape kept him true to its character and light. In his paintings of landscapes under the khamsin, which the late Edward Alden Jewell, writing of Rubin's exhibition in New York at the end of 1930, was to describe as "a whole fluid world swimming in light,"[20] he achieves a form of expression that is at once intensely personal and representationally accurate.

During these same years Rubin began to paint flower pieces, which he has continued to do ever since. These are among the most immediately enjoyable of his works. With his inborn feeling for decorative accents, he had introduced the flower motif into his paintings as early as 1921; his self-portraits of that year and the next (plate 90) show him either holding a jar with a flower in it or with a vase of flowers near him. In 1923 he painted the first of his *Flowers on My Window Sill,* a primitive forerunner of many variations on this theme, and in that year he also painted his first *Rider with Bouquet* (plate 91), in which a central motif is a large arrangement of brightly colored, stylized flowers, contrasting in lively manner with the muted color scheme. In these canvases, flowers are used as a decorative element of varying importance in the general composition, a device to which he would later return many times. In the late twenties, however, flowers became a theme in themselves. In conversation Rubin has said that he had always reveled in the color, shape, and

30 DUO PORTRAIT. 1954–60.
Oil on canvas, 16 × 13". Collection Mr. and
Mrs. Louis S. Kaplan, New York

31 Rubin with his wife, Esther,
in New York, 1967

58

32 ESTHER. 1942.
Oil on canvas, 10 × 9″.
The Rubin Museum Foundation

perfume of flowers, but that his interest in them as a main subject for a painting only arose after Esther's arrival in the country: they would return from their country-side outings with bunches of wild flowers, and she would carefully arrange them in bowls and vases in his home, so that he was always conscious of their beauty. At the time there were no cultivated flowers, except for those found in the few private gardens that existed. He delighted in painting mixed bouquets of poppies, yellow marguerites, and ears of corn; and anemones, which cover the fields with red, white, and purple in the early spring, became a particular favorite. He rendered these with a loving attention to naturalistic detail. Later, the mauve-blues of the iris, the blur of gold of the mimosa, the gamut of yellows and reds of the gerbera, and the contrast of white rose to deep-green leaf attracted him. With the years, his handling of flower pieces has grown freer, with more emphasis on vibrance of color than on shape of individual flowers, but he still keeps fairly close to nature. He has made of these flower pieces, painted with evident love and enjoyment, a joyful hymn to nature.

Rubin and Esther were married in March, 1930, and the day after the ceremony they left for a journey that was to take them from Egypt to Paris, thence to London, and then to New York, where the artist was to meet his wife's family for the first time. The London visit had been arranged to coincide with his first exhibition in that city. Here he showed mainly his recently painted landscapes with olive trees, and the exhibition was a critical, if not pecuniary, success. At the end of the summer the couple left for New York. New York was feeling the effects of the Depression, and Rubin recalls that the atmosphere of gloom affected him so strongly that he could not paint, although he had rented a pleasant studio and had planned to work. Funds were low and prospects for selling paintings discouraging, but his old friend in the New York art world, George Hellman, succeeded in arranging an exhibition for him at the Montross Gallery on Fifth Avenue for the month of December. This, like the London show, was artistically successful but financially not very rewarding, and at the end of 1930 he and Esther returned to Tel Aviv.

In the early thirties Rubin did not produce any large important canvases, and it was during these years that he took to watercolor. This side of his work is little known, since almost all such paintings were bought by collectors as soon as executed and have seldom been exhibited. And, except as washes for his colored drawings, he has not used this medium since. He is a delightful watercolorist, using clear, delicate washes of thin color with a sure hand. His subjects are similar to those of his oils—lyrical evocations of landscape, figure and animal studies, flower pieces—and, with their pale tonalities and tender color schemes, they are works of great charm and sensitivity (plate 42).

In 1931 he found another outlet for his creative talent in designing stage sets for the Habimah and for the workers' theater Ohel ("tent"). The following year was marked by the opening of the Tel Aviv Museum with a Rubin exhibition, a tribute to the position he had achieved as the country's leading painter. An art museum for the rapidly growing city of Tel Aviv had been a cherished project of its first mayor, Meir Dizengoff, and it would prove an important factor in the development of art in the country. It started off in a small way, however, with the exhibition galleries consisting of some rooms in the mayor's own house. The initial collection, donated by an Antwerp collector, contained some good examples of French and Belgian contemporary masters, including paintings by Pissarro, Ensor, Utrillo, and Vlaminck.

The opening was considered a significant cultural event, and large crowds thronged the building. Rubin had not held a solo exhibition in Tel Aviv since 1927, and the critics in general remarked on a new vivacity and luminosity in his work, while the well-known Hebrew writer Jacob Fichman, a lover of painting who occasionally wrote art criticism, noted a "search for new ways," and was particularly impressed by the landscapes which, he said, "reflect purity and a sense of holiness. They are the landscapes of a land awaiting the Messiah."[21]

During the following few years the painter spent much time traveling. He likes the feeling of being on the move and nearly always brings back sketchbooks filled with impressions and notes (plates 33, 34). He made his first visit to Petra in Trans-Jordan, the one-time capital of the Nabataeans, a city carved out of rose-colored rock; he went down to Aqaba on the Red Sea, noted for its vivid blue; he went to Jericho, near the Dead Sea, the lowest spot in the country, which is known as "the City of Palms," and is surrounded by orchards and much greenery; and he revisited Safed, Tiberias, and other favorite spots of his in Galilee.

While his wife went to New York to spend some months with her parents, Rubin took off for Europe, again to visit the museums of Italy, France, and Holland

33 BEDOUIN RACING IN EL ARISH. 1933. Brush and Chinese ink, 13 ½ × 19 ½".
Collection Esther Rubin, Tel Aviv

and to see what was taking place in the art world of the day. The deepest impression
of the tour was made by the works of Rembrandt he saw in Holland. And even today, over thirty-five years later, there is evident emotion in his voice as he describes
the effect *The Jewish Bride* in the Rijksmuseum had on him: ''A miracle of painting,
. . . of feeling in paint.'' So moved was he by this painting that when the guard was

34 THE ROAD TO SAFED. 1934. Pencil, 11 ½ × 16 ½".
Collection the artist, Tel Aviv

out of the gallery, he dared to caress the surface of the canvas with his hand. That the impact made by the Rembrandts was an enriching experience can be seen in the canvases of old Jews engaged in ritual observance that he painted over the next years. These include *Washing of the Hands* (1936; plate 35), *Crowning of the Torah* (1939; plate 36), and *Silent Prayer* (1942; plate 160). They are more deeply felt than

35 WASHING OF THE HANDS. 1936.
Oil on canvas, 42 × 35″.
Collection Mr. and Mrs. Edward G. Robinson,
Beverly Hills, Calif.

36 CROWNING OF THE TORAH. 1939.
Oil on canvas, 36 × 29″.
Collection Mr. and
Mrs. Fredric R. Mann, Philadelphia

his former figure compositions, as well as more emotional in brushstroke and warmer in color, and it is clear that it was not the pictorial aspects that he wanted to stress, but the spiritual.

The year 1936 witnessed the eruption of the most serious Arab riots since the Balfour Declaration, but the Jewish community did not allow these to interrupt the course of daily life or the efforts being made to build the country. It was in this year that the Palestine (now Israel) Philharmonic Orchestra was founded and that the house which the mayor of Tel Aviv had given for a museum was enlarged and adapted to this purpose. As his act of personal defiance, Rubin held two exhibitions at the time, one in Jerusalem and one in Tel Aviv, and he remembers that, unexpectedly, sales were good.

From the next couple of years date some of his finest landscapes, in which his interest in light and atmosphere, awakened at the beginning of the decade, is combined with compositions that are well thought-out and balanced. The description of what his eye had seen is tempered by his poetic imagination. The olive trees that to him were "the guardians of the landscape" continue to dominate the foreground, while the small figures of peasants at work do not disturb the general mood of tranquility (plate 152).

Flute Player (plate 46), which was later acquired by The Museum of Modern Art in New York, and a self-portrait later exhibited at the show "Twentieth-Century Portraits" at the same museum were both painted in 1938. The formalization and stylization of such earlier figure studies as *Portrait of Yehuda Goor* (1927; plate 129) and *Yemenite Boy* (1930; plate 140) have gone and are replaced by grace and a feeling for the natural and unaffected. Form and color have been integrated, and in the mauve-pinks and soft blues of *Flute Player* and the warm reds of the portrait there is a sensuousness in the use of paint that had not been seen previously.

In the same year the painter made two trips to London. Greatly stimulated by the theater, an interest going back to his days in Rumania, he had been instrumental in enlisting the support of Sir Arthur Wauchope, the British high commissioner, to build a playhouse for the Habimah Theater, for, although internationally known, the Habimah had no suitable hall in which to perform. Sir Arthur arranged for the requisitioning of a plot of land in Tel Aviv to house a cultural center; the first building was to be a theater for Habimah. In 1937, the theater management persuaded

Rubin to go to London to raise funds for the building, and the next year he returned to that city for his second successful exhibition at the Tooth Gallery. Also in 1938, he began to prepare for a requested exhibition in Rumania, which he had not visited since his last exhibition in Bucharest in 1924, and for two projects—the stage sets for an opera and a mural. The visit, on which he was to be accompanied by his wife, was set for the summer of 1939, but it was not to take place. The political situation in Europe was deteriorating rapidly, and Rubin felt this was not the time to go to Rumania. A complex personality, shrewd and practical, and at the same time romantic and a dreamer, he is much influenced by signs and portents, and he declares that his dreams at the time always contained references to disasters in the country of his birth. So the Rumanian visit was dropped but not the idea of travel and an exhibition abroad. The Rubins would go to America to spend a few months, and negotiations were started for a New York exhibition. In the meantime, an exhibition had been arranged to take place in Jerusalem at the Bezalel Museum in December, and when it closed the couple left for New York, little dreaming that their projected short stay would become a six-year sojourn, for the war that had begun in September grew continually in force and prevented their return to Palestine.

If the period in Rubin's life from the time of his settlement in Palestine to his departure for what was to be a prolonged stay in America has been dwelt on in detail, it is because the years from 1923 to 1939 were decisive for his development as an artist. It was during these years that he fused together the various methods of treating his themes with which he had experimented and the influences that he had, unconsciously, absorbed. By 1939 he was a mature artist who had evolved an individual style, a style that places him in the French tradition and yet, while acknowledging a certain debt to both Dufy and Renoir, is undeniably his own. By this time, he had acquired the ability to orchestrate color, and he had developed a confident touch in the manipulation of oil pigment, along with a linear grace, which, allied to his inborn aptitude for decorative composition, allowed him to give free expression to what he wished to communicate—fundamentally, then as now, a happy affirmation of life.

THE SIX years Rubin spent in America represent the longest period he has been away from the country of his choice. He has always claimed that he has felt himself a stranger everywhere except in Israel, and, while his stay in America brought him artistic and material success, established his reputation in that country, and gained him friendships that have continued till today, he always regarded himself as a visitor who would shortly return home.

During his stay he met and came to know many American artists and kept up with new trends by visiting galleries and museums, but he was never drawn to associate with one group or another. He is alert to new trends and tendencies, although he is not swayed by them; his instinct keeps him away from what does not suit his particular purpose. Not surprisingly, therefore, the change in milieu does not seem to have affected either his perception or his pictorial language, and it is from his American years that date such canvases as *Silent Prayer* and *Still Life with Fruit* (1941; plate 48). In this last, cherries have replaced the pomegranates in which he takes such delight. A California friend recalls visiting his studio and being struck by the many "glowing flower pieces" he painted when in Los Angeles.

During these years Rubin executed a number of portraits, although portraiture never interested him greatly, perhaps because he, as a painter who takes reality as his point of departure, prefers to be less tied to his subject than portrait painting allows. He has never accepted portrait commissions, and his sitters have always been personal friends and their children, or members of his own family. For children he has a special fondness, and his portraits of them have particular warmth and sympathetic understanding. In America he became friendly with people of the musical and theatrical world, and it was from these circles that his sitters were drawn. The author has not seen any of these original paintings, but from photographs of the portraits of the pianist Artur Rubinstein, the violinist Yehudi Menuhin, and the actor Sam Jaffe, for instance, it is clear that Rubin sought to emphasize individual characteristics.

Talking about this period of his life, Rubin has said, "I did paint skyscrapers and the Hudson River, but I never felt that these works represented the real me and they meant little to me." Questioned as to what became of these canvases, of which only one, *East River, New York*—a lyrical interpretation of the scene in which blues and grays predominate—has been shown in Israel, he has said that most of them were sold and he painted over the others.

37 Rubin receiving degree of
Doctor of Hebrew Letters from
Dr. Stephen S. Wise, Jewish Institute of Religion,
New York, 1945

Between the beginning of 1940 and the end of 1945, Rubin held six one-man shows and participated in the exhibition "Twentieth-Century Portraits" at The Museum of Modern Art in New York (1942). A touring exhibition of thirty of his paintings, arranged by the Council of Art Museums in cooperation with the Dalzell Hatfield Galleries of Los Angeles, was circuited through museums in the western states from 1944 to 1946. Critical reception was almost unanimously favorable. Typical were the comments of art critic Emily Genauer: ". . . a highly sensitive, original painter, whose work is moody and richly romantic—drenched with luminous tone and enveloped in the shimmering, arid atmosphere travelers tell us is characteristic of Palestine."[22]

In addition to *Flute Player,* acquired by the New York Museum of Modern Art, paintings were purchased by the museums of Los Angeles (County Museum), Santa Barbara, and San Antonio, Texas.

In the spring of 1945 took place one of the most important events in Rubin's personal life, the birth of his son, David, which illuminated the last year of his stay in America. In January of that same year he was awarded the honorary degree of Doctor of Hebrew Letters by the Jewish Institute of Religion in New York. In conferring the degree, the late Dr. Stephen Wise said:

> Rubin is the strong and joyous artist who has helped to create and has brought to the attention of the world a whole new world of art, the art of Palestine, its landscape, its trees and cities, its men and women. He has dedicated his life and genius to render in terms of visible beauty the miraculous renaissance of our people in Eretz Israel.
>
> With originality and with a style both subtle and splendid, he has painted the Hassidim of Safed, the Halutz of the Emek, the great intellectual leader Ahad Haam, the shepherds and fishermen of Galilee, the old and holy cities of Jerusalem and Safed, the new colonies in the Sharon valley, the ancient olive trees, the almond trees in blossom, and the glorious beauty of the field flowers in the hills of Judea. . . . This man has deserved well of the Jewish people.

The war was now drawing to a close, and the Rubins were awaiting the first opportunity to take ship for Palestine, which, however, they were unable to do until the spring of 1946.

THE FIRST months after the return to Palestine were a period of difficult readjustment and represented one of the rare times in Rubin's life when he could not settle down to paint. Since no apartment was available in Tel Aviv for the family, they went to Jerusalem, and, as so often in its history, the city was beset by troubles. As the seat of British power in the country, it was the target of attacks by dissident Jewish underground groups enraged by the refusal of the mandatory administration to allow the asylum-seeking Jews of Europe to enter the country. Shootings and bombings were frequent. It was impossible to work, and after a few months Rubin determined to move to Tel Aviv. He was able to secure an apartment in the heart of the city, and he started again to work and to prepare for an exhibition at the Tel Aviv Museum, which was held in May, 1947. Critical reaction was mixed. Even before Rubin left for America, changes had been taking place in art in Palestine—along with many other aspects of life in the country—and Rubin was criticized for not "projecting the reality of Palestine," for presenting it as a "land of sweet and earthly beauty—a joyful blend of brilliant flowers and beautiful costumes," and for not attempting to "wrestle with and create new values within the confines of his work."[23] On the other hand, he was praised for having "created a genre of his own, an identifiable Rubin idiom," for his "freshness and elegance," and for the "extraordinarily perceptive eye and sound draftsmanship" shown in his drawings.[24] The painter himself was unperturbed by praise or blame:

> The artist must be true to his convictions, to what he feels instinctively. What is news is not necessarily worthwhile. I must follow the dictates of my heart.
>
> If a painting of mine can add one iota to anyone's joy in living, then I feel I have succeeded.

On November 29, the General Assembly of the United Nations voted for the partition of Palestine between Jew and Arab, giving sovereignty to each. The Jewish community rejoiced; the Arabs brought a new intensity to the violence of their attacks. Jerusalem bore the brunt, but Tel Aviv endured sniping from nearby Jaffa day and night, and, until Jaffa capitulated to the Jewish fighters, the border between the two cities was a battleground for weeks. Then came May 14 and the declaration of the state of Israel.

All the time Rubin had continued to work steadily. He could have replied in a

38 Rubin directing the execution of
stage sets for *Day and Night*,
Habimah Theater, Tel Aviv, 1948

manner similar to Cézanne, who when once asked what he did in the war of 1870
answered: "Pendant la guerre, j'ai beaucoup travaillé sur le motif à l'Estaque."
During this period Rubin had a particular urge to work on light and colorful
themes, and some of his gayest flower pieces were painted then. He also made many
sketches of his three-year-old son sleeping and at play. It was in 1948 that he returned again to stage design, creating sets for both the Habimah and Ohel.

The declaration of the state of Israel brought with it a great, if temporary, change
in Rubin's life. He was appointed the first Minister Plenipotentiary to Rumania.
The proposal that he become a diplomat came as a complete surprise to the painter,
and at first he had misgivings about accepting. But the confidence in his abilities
expressed by the prime minister, Ben-Gurion, and the foreign minister, Moshe
Sharett, persuaded him that he did not have the right to refuse to serve his country.

39 Rubin in Bucharest as Minister
Plenipotentiary to Rumania, 1948

The appointment may have surprised Rubin, but not his friends and acquaint-
ances or even the community at large. He had long been a public figure, known not
only as the first of the country's painters to exhibit abroad and win outside recognition, but also as an active, energetic man associated with a number of communal
projects, and on friendly terms with many of Israel's leaders in various fields. His
is the type of forceful personality that attracts attention and creates legends; doubtless his arresting physical appearance also plays a role.

40 SWORD DANCER. 1924.
Pen and ink and crayon, 19 × 12 ½″.
Collection Mrs. R. Davis, New York

41 PORTRAIT OF A POET AND HIS WIFE.
1927. Oil on canvas, 36 × 28 ½″.
Collection Esther Rubin, Tel Aviv

42 MY WINDOW IN SAFED. 1930.
Watercolor, 15 ½ × 13″.
Collection Sarah Wilkinson,
Tel Aviv

43 LANDSCAPE NEAR SAFED. 1930. Watercolor, 13 × 15 ½″.
Collection Sarah Wilkinson, Tel Aviv

44 KHAMSIN IN GALILEE. 1934. Oil on canvas, 26 × 32″.
Israel Museum, Jerusalem

45 FISHERMEN IN TIBERIAS.
1937. Pen and ink and
gouache, 15 ½ × 12 ½″.
Binet Gallery, Tel Aviv

46 FLUTE PLAYER. 1938.
Oil on canvas, 36 × 32″.
The Museum of Modern Art,
New York

47 FAMILY AT REST. 1941. Pen and ink and gouache, 12 ½ × 17″.
Galerie Motte, Geneva

48 STILL LIFE WITH FRUIT. 1941. Oil on canvas, 29 × 36".
Collection Mr. and Mrs. Abraham Feinberg, New York

49 FISHERMAN FAMILY FIXING NETS. 1947. Pen and ink and wash, 20 × 26″.
Collection Mrs. R. Davis, New York

50 SNAKE CHARMER. 1950.
Mixed media, 20 × 14″.
Collection Ariella Rubin,
Tel Aviv

51 ABRAHAM GREETS THE THREE VISITORS. 1954. Pen and ink and wash, 22 ½ × 31″.
Collection Esther Rubin, Tel Aviv

52 FIRST SEDER IN JERUSALEM. 1950. Oil on canvas, 50 ½ × 64″.
The Rubin Museum Foundation

He has often said that returning to the country he had left as a poor, awkward youth, dreaming of becoming an artist, as a representative of the new state of Israel was an extraordinary experience that filled him with wonderment at the ways of fate. The whole period of his stay in Rumania had an aura of mystical significance for him.

Rubin spent eighteen months there, returning to Israel on the same ship that carried the first thousand immigrants whose exit permits he had been instrumental in obtaining.

He was happy to get back to his easel and paints and the normal life of a citizen of Tel Aviv. But that the "ingathering of the Jewish people," which had been one of his main tasks in Rumania, was still on his mind can be seen in the large *First Seder in Jerusalem* (plate 52), which dates from 1950. Around the table set for the traditional meal on the eve of Passover, which celebrates the Exodus from Egypt, are gathered immigrants from various parts of the world, with the officiating rabbi as the central figure. To the right are the painter himself and his son, holding a round of unleavened bread, and behind them, the artist's wife. An Arab also is included, in abaya, kaffiya, and agal (traditional Arab garments—cloak, headdress, and headband), while at the extreme left sits an ambiguous figure, gazing at his hands marked by stigmata, which also appear on his feet. Is he prophet or messiah? In the background, as in a quattrocento interior with figures, appear the walled city of Jerusalem and a range of mountains seen through arches. The composition is reminiscent of Leonardo's *Last Supper*. In this canvas, with its symbolism and its strong, simple draftsmanship and clearly defined figures, Rubin has reverted to his "naive" manner of painting of the early twenties, as if his principal aim here were not the creation of pictorial values but the presentation of a "document" of the period of mass immigration following the declaration of the state of Israel.

In the same year, 1950, he began to work on a new theme, of which he later made many variations: a scene with musical instruments. Apparently the visit of the violinist Jascha Heifetz, a personal friend, stimulated Rubin's interest in this subject matter. In May of that year, Heifetz was making his first appearance with the Israel Philharmonic Orchestra and, wanting quiet between his many concerts, arranged to live in the rural town of Rehovot, seat of the Weizmann Institute of Science, not far from Tel Aviv. There Rubin often visited him and, sitting in the music room,

53 QUARTET IN REHOVOT. 1951. Oil on canvas, 23 ½ × 32″.
Collection Mr. and Mrs. Seniel Ostrow, Beverly Hills, Calif.

54 MUSICAL INTERLUDE:
HOMAGE TO CASALS. 1964.
Oil on canvas, 36 × 29".
Norton Gallery, Palm Beach, Fla.
Gift of Regenstein Foundation

would look out through the widely opened doors at a landscape of orange groves and cypresses. From this scene, as it impressed itself on his memory, Rubin has created some of his most evocative paintings. Typical is *Quartet in Rehovot* (1951; plate 53), showing an empty room with the dark shapes of the musical instruments and chairs forming a pattern against a landscape filled with light. Light permeates the room, so that the whole painting seems to breathe the brightness of a summer day, and the sound of the music that has been played there seems to linger on. Other versions of the theme, painted much later, are freer both in conception and execution and show that, while Rubin constantly returns to the same themes, the way he approaches and handles them continually evolves. For example, in *Musical Interlude: Homage to Casals* (1964; plate 54), the foreground of the unconventional composition is dominated not only by the musical instruments but also by one of the artist's favorite motifs: a large vase filled with flowers. The nebulous background, with its antique columns, refers to Caesarea, the Roman capital of Palestine, in whose ancient amphitheater Casals played. Here too, an important feature is a group of olive trees, another of Rubin's loved motifs. These diverse elements have been combined to make a whole that symbolizes the mysterious power of music.

In the late spring of 1952, Rubin again left for New York with his family, with the avowed object of holding exhibitions. "I had been a dollar-a-year man as a diplomat and I felt the need to repay the debts incurred by this luxury." In November, his daughter, Ariella, was born, arriving on the painter's birthday. This happy event was a good augury for the stay, which proved successful in every way and enabled Rubin, on his return to Tel Aviv, to purchase the house in which he lived and to build a fine studio on the roof.

During 1953 and 1954, he held solo exhibitions in New York, Los Angeles, at the Mint Museum (Charlotte, North Carolina), and at the Parthenon in Nashville, Tennessee. He also participated in a group show of seven leading Israeli painters, selected and arranged by James S. Plaut, director of the Institute of Contemporary Art in Boston. The collection was shown at the Institute of Contemporary Art in January, 1953, then at Pittsburgh's Carnegie Institute, the Metropolitan Museum of Art in New York, and subsequently in other North American cities. Rubin was represented by twelve paintings, which included *Washing of the Hands* (plate 35), *Flute Player* (plate 46), and *Shepherd* (1950; plate 170). His work was singled out for special notice with such comments as: "unquestionably the most solidly accomplished of the group of seven Israeli artists. He has a strength of emotional evocation that indicates real artistic maturity."[25]

A number of paintings shown in this collection, such as *Washing of the Hands* and *Portrait of a Poet and His Wife* (1927; plate 41), were also shown at the Venice Biennale of 1952 when the Israel Pavilion was opened; Rubin was represented there by seventeen works.

By the beginning of 1955, Rubin was once more back in Tel Aviv and was soon engaged in preparing for a retrospective exhibition covering forty years of work, which was to be held at the Tel Aviv Museum in May. It brought together 123 oils, a number of watercolors and drawings, and also sculpture, woodcuts (*The God Seekers;* plates 23–25), and designs for the theater. It aroused wide interest and was hailed as "a national event," most critics agreeing with the critic of the *Jerusalem Post,* who wrote: "Rarely have we seen Israel so tremblingly alive and fresh as Rubin gives her to us."[26]

It was at this exhibition that *Goldfish Vendor* (1955; plate 61), later to be acquired by the Musée National d'Art Moderne in Paris, was first shown. It is interesting to compare the early version of the same subject, painted in 1926 (plate 60), with this work. Although the pose is almost the same in both, the interval of nearly thirty years had, as might be expected, wrought great changes in approach and execution. Faithfulness to the actual appearance of the model has been replaced by the play of imagination, and naive simplicity by a sophisticated, differentiated handling. The apparent facility with which such a canvas as that of 1955 has been painted often blinds people to the fact that this ease and grace were only obtained as a result of concentrated effort and unremitting work. Even today Rubin will make a number of preliminary drawings, as well as oil sketches, for a projected painting, although once he begins on the actual picture he usually carries it through rapidly.

The two years following his retrospective exhibition seem to have been relatively quiet, with Rubin enjoying domesticity while at the same time, as is his habit, painting steadily and also producing a number of large-scale drawings, mainly of roosters and horses in movement. Executed in pen-and-ink and wash, they form an original and attractive part of his work.

The end of 1956 saw him again making ready for an exhibition abroad, this time in London at the well-known O'Hana Gallery. It took place in May and June of

1957; drawings as well as oils were shown. Once more he was able to record a notable success, with laudatory reviews in which the personal stamp of his work received special notice: "highly individual style of painting . . . an artist who is entirely himself."[27]

The following year, a selection of his paintings was again shown in London at an exhibition of art from Israel arranged by the Arts Council of Great Britain.

Toward the end of the fifties Rubin began to be much occupied with horses running in the desert as a subject for painting. He says he was inspired by his visits to the Negev, the desert south land that since 1949 has been a part of Israel. He would watch from afar the Bedouin horsemen galloping across the wastes where once Abraham sojourned and where Hagar had wandered with Ishmael, and to him the distant riders would take on the appearance of Biblical figures (*Night Rider in the Desert,* 1965; plate 68). He was fascinated by the mysterious atmosphere of the desert, and in several canvases there is a strong element of fantasy. The paintings become poetic symphonies of color, imbued with an atmosphere of mysticism; unlike most of Rubin's work, they are not tranquil in spirit but filled with turbulence, as if the horses, now riderless, are driven onward by unknown forces. He uses color arbitrarily: the horses are in blues, while the background, with a huge moon, is in greens, or the horses are in reds and the background in purples. The horses are delineated by thin contour lines, but so masterly is Rubin's draftsmanship that the forms have real solidity.

Running or rearing horses with flying manes have continued to be a favorite subject.

In 1960, after an interval of more than thirty years, Paris again saw a collection of Rubin's paintings when he exhibited with a group of Israeli artists at the Musée National d'Art Moderne. He showed paintings executed between 1950 and 1959, and again his work drew special attention. Art critic Claude Roger-Marx noted approvingly that "his canvases escape the new conformism of New York or Paris,"[28] while the critic of *La Liberation* declared that the exhibition "revealed to us a great painter, . . . master of a precise draftsmanship and a knowing brush, rich in sensitivity."[29] Official recognition came with the acquisition by the Musée National d'Art Moderne of two paintings, *Goldfish Vendor* and *Pomegranates on My Window* (1958; plate 208).

During this year he was also working on a series of large pen-and-ink drawings with sepia wash, which was issued in Paris the following year as an album of twelve lithographs under the title of *Visages d'Israël* (plates 65, 66), with introductory essays by the eminent French art critic Florent Fels and the director of the Tel Aviv Museum, Dr. Haim Gamzu. The album was very well reviewed and was quickly taken up by collectors.

In 1962 he made a visit of several months to America, chiefly in connection with his exhibition at the noted Wildenstein Galleries in New York in October of that year. He had not exhibited in New York for nine years, and it was decided that this time the show should be in the form of a retrospective. It proved highly successful; opening day brought a queue of visitors that stretched into the street. Reviews, such as that in *The New York Times,* were appreciative: "These eloquently lyrical paintings of Israel's landscape, traditions, and inhabitants reflect fantasy and color and cover forty years by a gifted artist who can justly be considered the painter laureate of Israel."[30] Art critic Alfred Werner found a "striking synthesis of architectural strength and luxuriant color"[31] in the recent paintings, and Rubin was referred to as "Israel's greatest living artist."[32]

The New York exhibition was followed by similar retrospectives in Los Angeles and Tucson, Arizona. In the early part of 1963, Rubin returned to Tel Aviv.

This was the year of Rubin's seventieth birthday, which found him with energies undiminished, painting with his usual assiduity. When asked about his plans, he replied he would "continue to paint." His birthday was feted by his friends and family and brought a spate of newspaper articles. In this connection it may be of interest to quote from the French art critic Raymond Charmet:

Rubin represents the complete artist—painter, sculptor, man of the theatre, writer, man of action, diplomat—as were the men of the Renaissance. Coming from a people above all others unhappy, he knew how to conquer happiness and to express it in works of sovereign harmony. His example is, we may hope, a prophet for our times.[33]

The next year, the city of Tel Aviv, of which he had been a leading citizen for forty years, awarded him a prize for a "lifetime's artistic achievement."

Rubin's seventieth birthday brought no decrease in his activities; rather, it brought an intensification. The following years, 1964 and 1965, are notable for the

Opposite:
56 Rubin at seventy with his family in the Tel Aviv studio, 1963

55 Moshe Dayan congratulating Rubin on his seventieth birthday, Tel Aviv, 1963

number of paintings produced—landscapes, figure compositions, flower pieces, and still lifes with pomegranates, often placed near an open window with a view beyond. It was also at this time that he painted a number of versions of *Abraham and the Three Angels* (plate 231) and began to make studies for themes on the life of King David. For these works he used much brighter color, with vibrant yellows and blues—colors he had seldom used in strength previously. From the same years also date his "stormy" landscapes, showing olive trees with twisted trunks lifting their bare branches to a livid sky, painted with a palette restricted to yellowy-greens and whites. They are unusual for Rubin, who generally prefers to depict nature in a happy mood, and whose idealized landscapes of the country show a land that seems always to be sleeping in a golden afternoon.

During this period, Rubin was also much occupied with the planning of the house he had decided to build in Caesarea on a plot of land facing the Mediterranean, overlooking the old Roman aqueduct. This was the realization of an old dream. As a youth, in a poem entitled "Fantasia," he had written:

> By the sea
> Lies my palace
> Dipping its feet
> In foaming waves
> Now green, now blue,
> Gathering, chasing
> None knows whence or whither.
>
> I long and yearn
> For what must be on the way
> Yet do not know
> Whether indeed it comes.

The "palace," a white, Mediterranean-style villa, for the garden of which Rubin was to bring olive trees from Galilee, palm trees from Deganiya on the shores of Lake Kinneret, and stones quarried in the Negev, was not ready for occupancy until 1966, but almost immediately after the first building stones were laid, Caesarea and its Roman remains became an important motif in many paintings.

In 1965 he made his first design for a tapestry, which was woven in Nazareth. For subject he chose *La Pêche Miraculeuse,* depicting a Neptune-like figure holding a net filled with fish (plate 237). The color scheme is mainly deep blues, relieved by passages in rose, white, and green. Since he had no experience in working with weavers and, it must be admitted, little faith in their capacity to carry out his design faithfully, he painted a meticulously detailed rendering of the design exactly the same size as the projected tapestry. A second design, commissioned by the new weaving atelier in Jerusalem called Jerusalem Tapestries, has now been completed. For this he chose a Biblical subject, *Jacob and the Angel* (plate 71), with a more complicated color scheme and composition than the first. In both designs he has adhered to the type of monumental figure composition of his paintings, using, however, stronger color contrasts, on the assumption that the passage of years will have a mellowing influence. In the same year he started to work on a large landscape, *Glory of Galilee,* commissioned for the Knesset (parliament), Jerusalem, which now hangs in the Cabinet chamber (plates 75, 238).

In May, 1966, the new Israel Museum in Jerusalem gave Rubin a large retrospective exhibition, which was later shown at the Tel Aviv Museum. Rubin had not held a one-man show in Jerusalem for nearly three decades, and he said at the time how moved he had been to be the first Israeli painter to hold a solo exhibition in the fine new museum and to have the opportunity to shake hands again with the people who had been present at his first exhibition in Jerusalem at the Tower of David over forty years before.

The invitation must be taken as a tribute to a veteran artist who not only "forms an organic part of the young history of Israel art which dates back to the early twenties,"[34] but one who "belongs to this history as a *living* artist, who pays daily creative homage in his workshop where there is waged the struggle between imaginative conception and execution."[35] It was undoubtedly also a recognition of the fact that Rubin was not only the first of the country's painters whose works were acquired for museums and important collections in Europe and America, but that he continues to be Israel's most internationally known painter.

This retrospective collection clearly revealed not only the extent of Rubin's achievement but also the changes that had taken place in his method of painting. Evident was the breakaway by the end of the twenties from the so-called Douanier

57 Rubin practicing yoga

Rousseau period, the subsequent interest in light and atmospheric effects that led to paintings of this period often being termed "Impressionist," and then the fusion of passion for light with carefully composed composition which, by the end of the thirties, resulted in the formation of his mature style, the style that is so immediately recognizable as Rubinesque. Since that time changes may have been slight, but they have taken place. By the end of the forties his color harmonies begin to show a much greater use of greens, doubtless due to the influence of the countryside, and by the fifties his compositions have become more open and less tight, with the abstract elements more pronounced. Rubin is not a painter who works to a formula, nor does he adhere strictly to one manner in any period, so that it is difficult to state categorically that his manner changed from any particular date.

In December of 1966 Rubin held his first exhibition in Switzerland, at the Galerie Motte in Geneva. Here he showed paintings executed in the sixties, including the *Landscape of Galilee* (1962; plate 67) and *Boy with Bouquet* (1966; plate 69), in which one color, green, is used to unify the painting. In the early spring of the next year, 1967, he held an exhibition at Palm Beach, Florida, at the Norton Gallery. Paintings from the late fifties and sixties were shown, nearly all of which were acquired by American collectors.

In the next couple of years Jewish subjects were again a main preoccupation, and from this time date several canvases with such titles as *Simhat Torah* (plate 70), *Rabbi with Torah* (plate 240), and *Musicians,* depicting orthodox Jews in traditional garb. These canvases are less monumental than his earlier works on the same subjects, as if he wanted to convey an ethereal spirituality. The figures are lightly delineated by white contour lines, and the pigment is applied in a particularly soft, even feathery manner. An exception is the forceful *Divine Spirit Returns to Jerusalem* (1967; plate 243). This was painted in the mood of elation after the Six-Day War and shows a blue-robed Hassid holding a Scroll of the Law; with head thrown back in ecstasy, he is sailing over a dreamlike Jerusalem of pale gold.

The ending of the war also drew from him an expressive *Peace Offering* (1967; plate 59), in which a father carrying a white lamb on his shoulder, a mother, and child are symbolically grouped together. Into the predominantly cold color scheme, a touch of warmth is introduced by the dish of crimson pomegranates held by the mother. This is a theme of which Rubin has made several versions over the years, but seldom with such a feeling of assured serenity.

58 Rubin with his daughter, Ariella, and his portrait of her in the Tel Aviv studio, 1968

59 PEACE OFFERING. 1967.
Oil on canvas, 36 × 29″.
Collection Mr. and Mrs. Walter Artzt,
New York

60 GOLDFISH VENDOR. 1926.
Oil on canvas, 29 × 24″.
Collection Mr. and
Mrs. Harold Ruttenberg, Pittsburgh

61 GOLDFISH VENDOR. 1955.
Oil on canvas, 42 × 28″.
Musée National d'Art Moderne, Paris

62 THE ROAD TO SAFED. 1951. Oil on canvas, 23 ¾ × 29″.
Collection Mr. and Mrs. David M. Heyman, New York

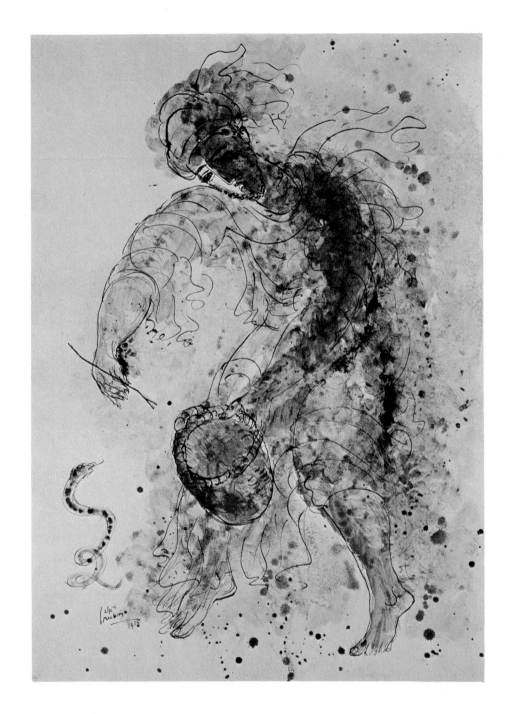

63 SNAKE CHARMER. 1956. Pen and ink and wash, 31 × 21 ½″.
Collection the artist, Tel Aviv

64 SNAKE CHARMER. 1957. Mixed media, 20 × 12 ½″.
Collection Ami Ginegar, Tel Aviv

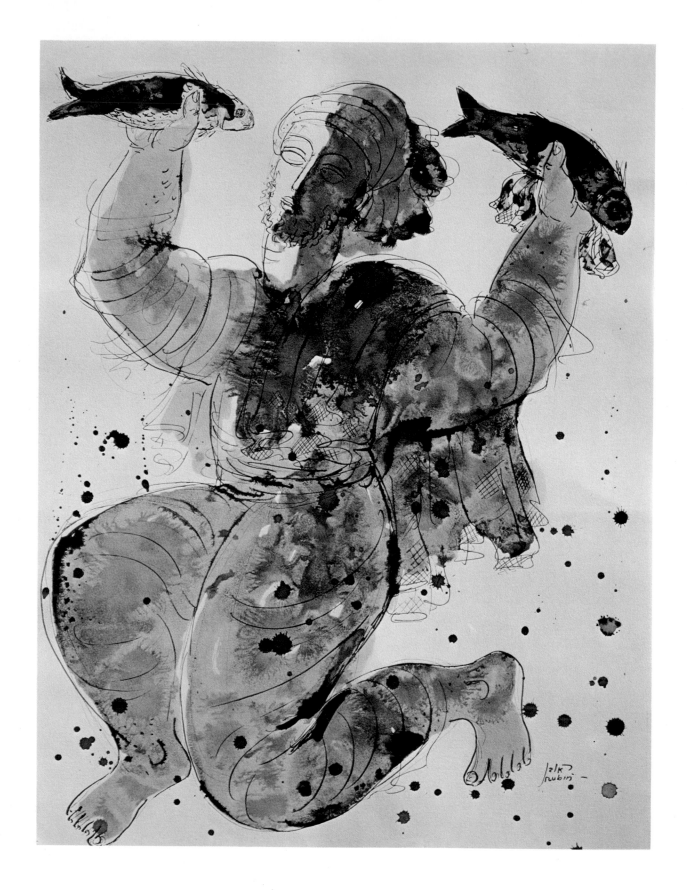

65 GALILEAN FISHERMAN. 1957.
Pen and ink, 26 × 20″.
Drawing for *Visages d'Israël,*
album of twelve lithographs
published by Daniel Jacomet,
Paris, 1961

66 THE STALLION. 1957. Pen and ink, 20 × 26″.
Drawing for *Visages d'Israël,* album of twelve lithographs
published by Daniel Jacomet, Paris, 1961

67 LANDSCAPE OF GALILEE. 1962. Oil on canvas, 15 × 18″.
Petit Palais, Geneva

68 NIGHT RIDER IN THE DESERT. 1965. Oil on canvas, 29 × 36″.
Collection Mr. and Mrs. Theodore Pollock, New York

69 BOY WITH BOUQUET. 1966.
Oil on canvas, 36 × 25″.
Collection Mr. and Mrs. Jack Resnick,
New York

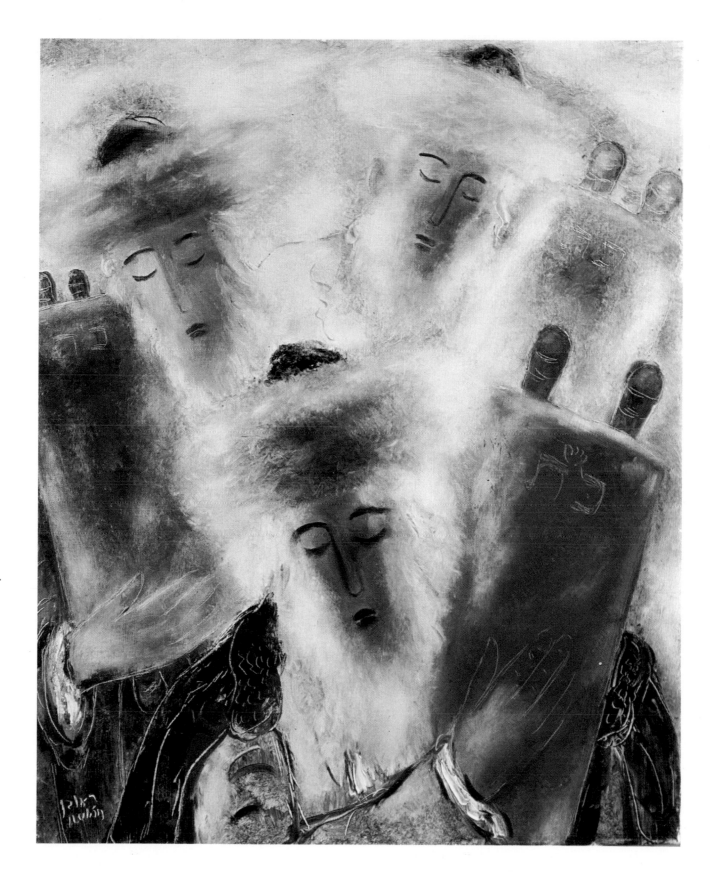

70 SIMHAT TORAH. 1967.
Oil on canvas, 32 × 26″.
Collection Mr. and Mrs.
Leslie Jackson, London

71 JACOB AND THE ANGEL. 1970.
Gouache, 39 ½ × 27 ½".
Design for tapestry.
Collection Mr. and Mrs. Sidney Baer,
Philadelphia

For some time Rubin had been contemplating writing some biographical sketches. He is a lively storyteller, with a remarkable memory and a droll turn of phrase, and he was constantly being urged by his friends to make a book of the episodes he recounted from his colorful and eventful life. In 1968 he finally set about doing it, and some eighteen months later *My Life, My Art* was published. Rubin insists that he is "a painter and not a writer," but in this story of a child of the Rumanian ghetto who aspired to be an artist and made his dream come true, he has produced memoirs that are both truly moving and richly humorous and that well merit their success.

The house at Caesarea is a great joy to Rubin, a retreat to which he can escape from the pressures of busy, noisy Tel Aviv to refresh his spirit in the unspoiled beauty of the stretch of land by the sea. It is there that he is seen at his most benign, feeding his white doves or wandering under his own palm trees, and bringing back roses and gerbera from the garden to his already flower-filled house.

72 Rubin working in the garden at Caesarea, 1967

73 Rubin feeding doves in Caesarea

74 Rubin with his wife, Esther, in the garden of their Caesarea home, 1966

75 Rubin working on
GLORY OF GALILEE
for the Knesset, Jerusalem, 1966

110

HEUREUX, QUI, COMME ULYSSE, A FAIT UN BEAU VOYAGE

DU BELLAY   "Sonnet XXXI"

I N A LIFE in which many honors and much prestige and appreciation have come his way, little has afforded Rubin more satisfaction than the planting of a forest in his name to mark his seventy-fifth birthday. The National Fund for Israel, with the participation of the painter's friends, planted twenty-five thousand trees in the hills of Jerusalem, and surely no greater or more gratifying homage could be paid by a people to an artist who loves and glorifies its country's landscape.

In his seventy-seventh year Rubin is painting with as much delight and vigor and as steadily as ever. From early in the morning until the afternoon he is closed in his studio. Nobody is permitted to enter during these hours. The landscape of Israel—its hillside villages, its trees, its flowers—enchants him as much now as it did when he first settled in the country nearly fifty years ago, and to his eyes the peasant women, shepherds, fishermen still maintain the Biblical aura with which he first invested them. If anything, the element of idealization in his blend of fantasy and lyrical realism has become more pronounced. His recent paintings of Jerusalem show a heavenly city, airy, floating in light, a mirage depicted in seductively pale colors; his landscapes with their olive trees are sunk even deeper into tranquility and his flower pieces are even more exuberant in color.

Rubin has lived through many changes in the world of art, seen many trends quickly hailed as of vital importance and then as quickly forgotten, and many ''isms'' that have come and gone, and he has had the strength not to succumb to any of them. He found his artistic personality many years ago, and he has always remained true to it. His instinct and his background led him to Israel, and a consuming love of his country and his people has sustained him ever since and has inspired him with the themes that he has been able lovingly to express in imagery of grace and harmony.

76 Rubin and his wife, Esther, with Tel Aviv Mayor Mordecai Namir, at planting of Rubin Forest in hills of Jerusalem, on the artist's seventy-fifth birthday, 1968

RUBIN AS DRAFTSMAN

WIDELY recognized as a brilliant draftsman, Rubin is an artist for whom drawing is not merely the first stage of a painting but a means of expression in itself. Whether he uses pen, pencil, or brush he is a master of line—line that is flowing, rhythmical, graceful, and yet strong and confident—and it is through his graphic work that he has found some of his most direct and forceful means of expression.

With a fluent and sure line he can describe the contours of a body, and with sparse, nervous strokes of a pen charged with energy he can magically convey movement, while out of an interplay of lightly and strongly stressed strokes he can vividly conjure up a landscape. He has said that he cannot remember a time when he did not draw, and even now he carries a sketchbook with him and still draws much from nature. Writing of an exhibition of Rubin's drawings held in New York in 1953, art critic Emily Genauer said: "His economical line is full of surging, rhythmic, dynamic movement, yet simultaneously so perceptive and sensitive as to bring to mind nothing less than certain sketches by Rembrandt."[36]

Rubin's preferred subject is the human figure, be it the majestic personages of the

77 PRANCING HORSES.
1968. Pastel and wash,
13 × 10″.
Private collection,
Jerusalem

78 TO MY POEM "GO!" 1917.
Ink and pencil, 10 ½ × 8 ½".
Collection the artist, Tel Aviv

79 CHAD GADYA. 1969.
Pen and ink, 14 × 10".
From *An Israel Haggadah* (adapted by Meyer Levin),
published by Harry N. Abrams, Inc.,
New York, 1969

Bible or the earthy figure of a peasant woman with a child in her arms, a fisherman throwing his net, or a shepherd of Galilee. The Arab woman gleaning corn could be Ruth in the field of Boaz, and the fisherman with his arms outflung in a wide gesture could be Moses casting down the tablets of stone, and the mother cradling her child in her arms could be the Virgin Mary. "Two thousand years ago or today, it matters little—for the artist whose real motive force is deep affection, today and yesterday are as one," wrote the English art critic Eric Newton.[37]

It is in these figure compositions, with their Biblical aura, that Rubin, at his best—when eye, hand, and heart are fully engaged—attains his most satisfying expression of natural harmony.

Rubin's early drawings of the twenties, made after he settled in Palestine, which in addition to figures include numerous animal studies, are in a more naturalistic manner. But his handling soon became lighter and more spontaneous, and he created a series of much-prized drawings. Notable is his treatment of the sinuous lines of the camel's body, reminiscent in rhythm of the undulating hills of Judea and Galilee. His sketchbooks of the thirties contain many fine studies of olive trees, some

80 JACOB AND THE ANGEL. 1966.
Wrought iron.
Collection the artist, Caesarea

81 YEMENITE FIANCÉS. 1935.
Pencil, 14 ½ × 10 ½″.
Collection the artist, Tel Aviv

82 MAESTRO TOSCANINI IN REHEARSAL. 1936.
Brush and Chinese ink, 17 × 12 ½″.
Collection Esther Rubin, Tel Aviv

executed with great exactitude of detail and others more impressionistic, with the light playing over the leafy branches. Toward the beginning of the fifties Rubin added to his animal drawings a series of roosters, usually with wings outspread, and horses running in the desert. Here he stressed not only movement but the over-all pictorial design and introduced thin washes of ink and color, achieving his personal synthesis of delicacy and bravura. At about the same time, as if by accident, he discovered the decorative possibilities of a splatter of ink drops, which has since become a Rubin characteristic.

Attracted by the revival of interest in lithography, in 1961 he created for Jacomet of Paris a set of twelve colored drawings, *Visages d'Israël,* for transference to lithographic stone. These won high acclaim and are notable for their refinement of line. Rubin's gift for evoking a ''serene and tender atmosphere'' is pointed out by the French art critic Florent Fels, in his preface to the album. He also remarks on Rubin's ability to give ''sublimity to his personages'' and writes that ''the Bible, with its inspired lyricism, lives again after two thousand years, thanks to the poetic realism of Rubin.''

NOTES

1. Henri Matisse, ''Notes of a Painter,'' *Grande Revue*, 25 December 1908.

2. Reuven Rubin, ''I Find Myself,'' *Menorah Journal* (New York), October 1926.

3. Reuven Rubin, *My Life, My Art,* New York: Funk and Wagnalls, Sabra Books, 1969, p. 93.

4. Rubin, ''I Find Myself.''

5. *New York World,* November 1921.

6. *New York American,* November 1921.

7. *The New York Times,* November 1921.

8. *Sunday World,* 30 October 1921.

9. M. Asch, ''Rubin's Exhibition,'' *Doar Hayom* (Jerusalem), 21 March 1923.

10. Eugene Kolb, introduction to ''Rubin Retrospective'' (catalogue), Tel Aviv Museum, May 1955.

11. ''Rubin Exhibition,'' *Palestine Weekly,* 14 March 1924.

12. ''Rubin's Exhibition,'' *Haaretz* (Tel Aviv), 12 March 1924.

13. Eric Newton, foreword to ''Rubin'' (catalogue), London, O'Hana Gallery, May–June, 1957.

14. Rubin, ''I Find Myself.''

15. Yona Fischer, ''Painting,'' in *Art in Israel,* ed. B. Tammuz and M. Wykes-Joyce, Tel Aviv: Massadah, 1965, p. 19.

16. Eric Newton, foreword to ''Rubin.''

17. *Chroniques et Documents,* June 1928.

18. Rubin, *My Life, My Art,* pp. 186, 189.

19. *Evening Standard* (London), 8 May 1930.

20. *The New York Times,* 21 December 1930.

21. ''The Rubin Exhibition,'' *Moznaim* (Tel Aviv), 14 May 1932.

22. *New York World Telegram,* 4 May 1941.

23. A. Kalb, ''Rubin's Exhibition at the Tel Aviv Museum,'' *Ha'Olam Hazeh* (Tel Aviv), May 1947.

24. Haim Gamzu, ''Rubin Exhibition at the Tel Aviv Museum,'' *Haaretz,* 26 May 1947.

25. Robert M. Coates, *New Yorker,* 23 June 1953.

26. Sara Moshkovitz-Varkonyi, ''Rubin Retrospective,'' *Jerusalem Post,* 3 June 1955.

27. Oswell Blakestone, *Apollo* (London), June 1957.

28. Claude Roger-Marx, *Le Mois à Paris,* May 1960.

29. *La Liberation,* 21 April 1960.

30. *The New York Times,* 6 October 1962.

31. Alfred Werner, *Jewish News,* 12 October 1962.

32. *New York Daily Mirror,* 7 October 1962.

33. *Arts* (Paris), 14 November 1963.

34. Haim Gamzu, introduction to ''Rubin Retrospective'' (catalogue), Israel Museum, Jerusalem, and Tel Aviv Museum, Spring 1966.

35. Haim Gamzu, introduction to ''Rubin Retrospective.''

36. *New York Herald Tribune,* 19 December 1953.

37. Eric Newton, foreword to ''Rubin.''

PLATES

83 MY FATHER AND MOTHER. 1916. Pen and ink and wash, 24 × 17 ½″.
Collection the artist, Tel Aviv

84 MY MOTHER. 1922. Pen and ink and wash, 19 × 12 ½″.
Collection Isaac Zelicovici, Tel Aviv

85 TEL AVIV. 1912. Oil on canvas, 21 ½ × 29 ½".
Collection Ayala Zacks, Toronto and Tel Aviv

86 TEL AVIV SEASHORE. 1920. Oil on canvas, 22 × 23″.
Collection Mr. and Mrs. A. Polany, Tel Aviv

87 THE MILKMAN. 1920.
Oil on canvas, 30 × 26".
Collection Esther Rubin,
Tel Aviv

88 PROCESSION WITH TORAH. 1921.
Oil on canvas, 36 × 29″.
Collection Esther Rubin, Tel Aviv

89 SHEEP SHEARER. 1923. Oil on canvas, 25 ½ × 25 ½".
Collection Mr. and Mrs. Aba Elhanani, Tel Aviv

90 SELF-PORTRAIT WITH FLOWER. 1922. Oil on canvas, 38 × 24".
The Rubin Museum Foundation

91 RIDER WITH BOUQUET. 1923.
Oil on canvas, 32 × 26".
Collection Horace Richter, New York

92 FIRST FRUITS. 1923. Oil on canvas, 71 × 82″. The Rubin Museum Foundation

94 SELF-PORTRAIT. 1924. Pen and ink, 8 × 8″.
Collection the artist, Tel Aviv

93 MY PARENTS. 1922. Pencil, 10 ½ × 8″.
Collection Professor and Mrs. Mordecai Nadav, Jerusalem

95 STILL LIFE WITH PAPER FLOWERS.
1924. Oil on canvas, 29 × 24″.
Collection Esther Rubin, Tel Aviv

96 RAMPARTS OF JERUSALEM. 1924.
Oil on canvas, 24 × 29″.
Collection Professor and
Mrs. Yigael Yadin, Jerusalem

97 EREV SHABBAT IN SAFED. 1924.
Oil on canvas, 29 × 36″.
Collection Mr. and Mrs. Jack Resnick,
New York

98 JERUSALEM FAMILY. 1924.
Oil on canvas, 36 × 29″.
Collection Esther Rubin, Tel Aviv

99 FALSE PROPHETS. 1920.
Oil on canvas, 43 ½ × 38″.
Grosvenor Gallery, London

100 SOPHIE. 1924.
Oil on canvas, 32 × 26″.
Collection Mr. and Mrs.
D. Edgar Cohn, Malibu, Calif.

101 MOURNING WOMEN. 1924.
Pen and ink, 11 ½ × 14″.
Collection the artist, Tel Aviv

102 THE SEA OF GALILEE. 1924.
Oil on canvas, 21 × 29″.
Israel Museum, Jerusalem

103 OLD JERUSALEM. 1925. Oil on canvas, 31 × 39″.
The Rubin Museum Foundation

104 JAFFA. 1926.
Oil on canvas, 25 × 20″.
Collection Mr. and
Mrs. Laurence Hamilton,
Claremont, Calif.

105 SAFED IN GALILEE. 1925. Oil on canvas, 29 × 36".
Collection Mr. and Mrs. Leon Gildesgame, Mt. Kisco, N.Y.

108 SELF-PORTRAIT. 1925. Brush and ink, 20 × 13″.
Collection the artist, Tel Aviv

106 BACKGAMMON PLAYERS. 1925. Pen and ink, 14 × 15″.
Collection the artist, Tel Aviv

107 TO THE MARKET. 1925. Pencil, 9 × 13″.
Collection the artist, Tel Aviv

109 OLD JERUSALEM. 1926. Oil on canvas, 25 ½ × 32″.
Collection Nathan Cummings, New York

110 SELF-PORTRAIT (in Tel Aviv). 1925.
Oil on canvas, 32 × 26″.
Collection Mr. and Mrs. B. Weinberg, Paris

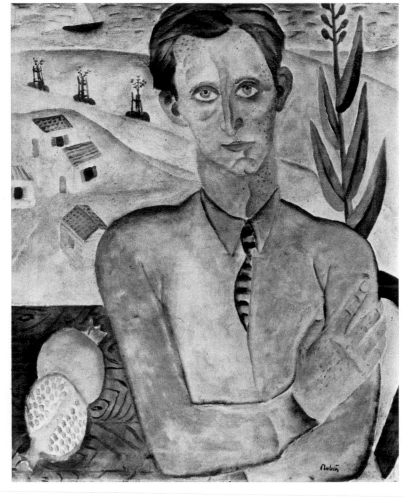

111 SUCCOTH IN JERUSALEM. 1925. Oil on canvas, 64 × 50 ½″.
The Rubin Museum Foundation

112 PORTRAIT OF THE POET URI ZVI GRINBERG. 1925.
Oil on canvas, 25 ½ × 21″. Tel Aviv Museum

113 EIN KAREM. 1926. Oil on canvas, 26 × 39″.
Collection Mr. and Mrs. Cecil Hyman, Jerusalem

114 ROAD TO SAFED. 1927. Oil on canvas, 29 × 36″.
Collection Hope Weil, New York

115 *(right)* OLD WALLS OF JERUSALEM. 1926.
Oil on canvas, 26 × 32".
Collection V. Van Vriesland, Jerusalem

116 *(bottom left)* IN GALILEE. 1927.
Pen and ink, 9 × 12".
Collection the artist, Tel Aviv

117 *(bottom right)* LANDSCAPE IN GALILEE
WITH ROMAN RUINS.
1927. Pen and ink, 9 × 12".
Collection the artist, Tel Aviv

118 ABRAHAM RECEIVES THE ANGELS. 1926.
Pen and ink and wash on
Chinese paper, 17 × 12 ½″.
Collection the artist, Tel Aviv

119 PORTRAIT OF FAITH. 1928.
Oil on canvas, 32 × 26″.
Collection Hope Weil, New York

148

Opposite:

120 *(top left)* IN THE SINAI. 1926.
Pencil, 14 × 11″.
Collection the artist, Tel Aviv

121 *(bottom left)* GOATS. 1927.
Pencil, 12 × 16″.
Collection the artist, Tel Aviv

122 *(top right)* CAMEL DRIVER. 1927.
Pen and sepia, 22 × 19″.
Collection Mrs. Ida Kimche, Caesarea

123 *(bottom right)* RELUCTANT CAMEL.
1928. Pencil, 10 ½ × 14 ½″.
Collection Mr. and
Mrs. David Rubin, Tel Aviv

124 JAFFA FISHERMAN FAMILY. 1927.
Oil on canvas, 32 × 26″.
Collection Mr. and Mrs. David
Lloyd Kreeger, Washington, D.C.

125 OLD JAFFA HARBOR. 1928. Oil on canvas, 26 × 32″.
Collection Mr. and Mrs. David Rubin, Caesarea

126 ʜᴀʀᴠᴇꜱᴛ ᴛɪᴍᴇ. 1931. Pen and ink, 13 ½ × 16 ½″.
Collection the artist, Tel Aviv

127 THE SEVEN MILLS. 1926.
Oil on canvas, 23 ½ × 32″.
Tel Aviv Museum

128 TIBERIAS ON THE SEA OF GALILEE. 1927.
Oil on canvas, 26 × 32″.
Collection Mr. and Mrs. Sam Aldock,
Washington, D.C.

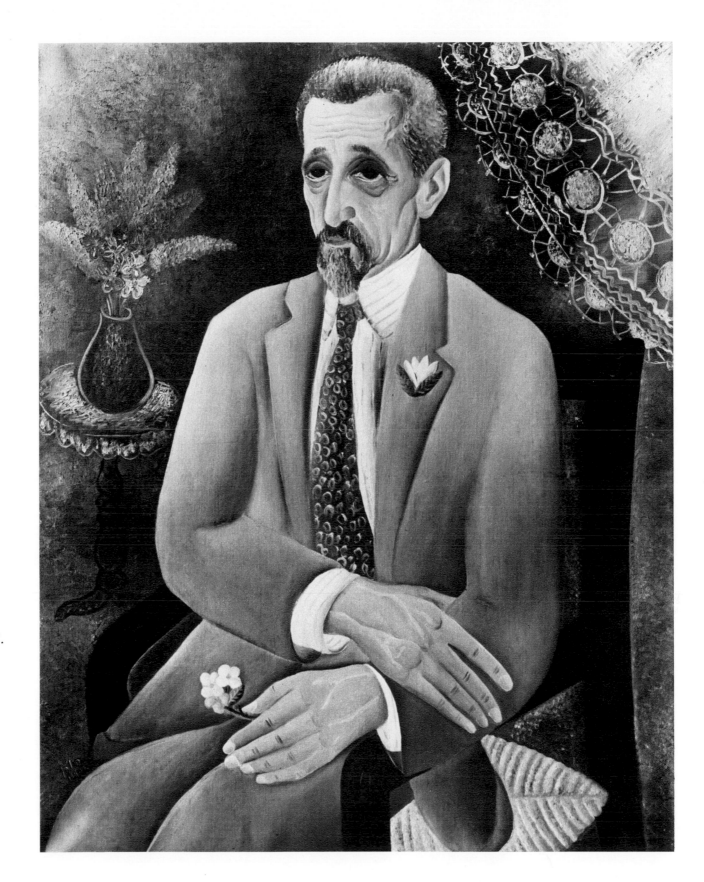

129 PORTRAIT OF YEHUDA GOOR. 1927.
Oil on canvas, 36 × 29″.
Collection Mr. and
Mrs. Asaph Goor, Jerusalem

130 BOY WITH FISH. 1928.
Pen and ink and wash, 22 ½ × 15 ½″.
Collection Esther Rubin, Tel Aviv

131 PORTRAIT OF SUZY. 1928.
Oil on canvas, 32 × 26″.
Collection Mildred Otto, New York

132 OLD OLIVE TREE IN SAFED. 1928. Pencil, 16 × 11″.
Collection the artist, Tel Aviv

133 RUTH. 1931. Pen and ink and wash, 13 ½ × 16″.
Collection the artist, Tel Aviv

156

134 OLD SYCAMORES. 1927. Oil on canvas, 26 × 32″.
Collection Pauline Polk, Claremont, Calif.

135 WHITE BOUQUET. 1929. Oil on canvas, 32 × 26″.
Collection Lord and Lady Powerscourt, Dublin

136 JAFFA HARBOR. 1931. Oil on canvas, 26 × 32″.
Private collection, New York

137 LES FIANCÉS. 1929.
Oil on canvas, 39 × 32″.
The Rubin Museum Foundation

159

138 GIRL WITH A DOVE. 1929.
Oil on canvas, 36 × 26″.
The Rubin Museum Foundation

139 FAMILY OF SAFED I. 1929.
Oil on canvas, 36 × 28 ½″.
Collection Mrs. Rose Klorfein,
New York

140 YEMENITE BOY. 1930.
Oil on canvas, 29 × 22".
Collection Mr. and Mrs. M. Mayer,
Geneva and Tel Aviv

141 MOTHER AND CHILD. 1932.
Pen and ink and pencil, 12 × 9 ½″.
Collection the artist, Tel Aviv

142 *(top right)* ABU KEBIR. 1931.
Oil on canvas, 20 × 24″.
Collection Mr. and Mrs. M. Mayer,
Geneva and Tel Aviv

143 *(bottom right)* JERUSALEM. 1934.
Oil on canvas, 28 × 35 ½″.
Collection Mrs. Jacob Sincoff, New York

144 SAFED IN THE HILLS OF GALILEE. 1936. Watercolor, 13 × 15 ½".
Collection Harold B. Cohen, New York

145 SELF-PORTRAIT. 1934.
Oil on canvas, 13 × 11″.
Collection Mr. and Mrs. Walter Artzt,
New York

146 JACOB'S DREAM. 1932. Oil on canvas, 32 × 23 ½".
Collection Mr. and Mrs. Astorre Mayer, Milan

147 FISHER FAMILY II. 1935. Pen and ink and wash, 25 ¼ × 19 ½".
Dalzell Hatfield Galleries, Los Angeles

148 GALILEE. 1935.
Oil on canvas, 24 × 32″.
Collection Mr. and Mrs. M. W. Weisgal,
Rehovot and Tel Aviv

149 PICKING OLIVES. 1936.
Oil on canvas, 26 × 32″.
Collection Cary Grant,
Beverly Hills, Calif.

150 THE ROAD TO BETHLEHEM. 1937. Oil on canvas, 21 × 29″.
Philadelphia Museum of Art

151 JERUSALEM FROM THE MOUNT OF OLIVES. 1937.
Oil on canvas, 29 × 36″.
San Antonio Museum, Texas
(First Purchase Prize)

152 HARVEST TIME IN NAZARETH. 1937.
Oil on canvas, 35 ½ × 42″.
Collection Mr. and Mrs. S. Cooke,
Wyncote, Pa.

153 FISHERMAN THROWING NET. 1938.
Pen and ink, crayon,
and gouache, 26 × 20″.
Collection Esther Rubin, Caesarea

154 EARLY MORNING IN GALILEE. 1937. Oil on canvas, 45 × 64″.
Collection Mr. and Mrs. David Lloyd Kreeger, Washington, D.C.

155 MUSICIANS OF SAFED. 1937. Oil on canvas, 36 × 29".
Collection Lord Sieff of Brimpton, London

156 KING DAVID DANCING BEFORE THE ARK. 1941.
Pen and ink and wash, 15 ½ × 12 ½".
Collection Mr. and Mrs. Nicolas Chapro, Beverly Hills, Calif.

157 IN THE JUDEAN HILLS. 1938. Oil on canvas, 20 × 28 ½″.
Collection Mr. and Mrs. D. Bunim, New York

158 AUTUMN BOUQUET. 1939. Oil on canvas, 26 × 32″.
Collection Mr. and Mrs. Frank Altschul, Stamford, Conn.

159 JACOB AND THE ANGEL. 1941.
Pen and ink and gouache, 17 × 12 ½".
Collection the artist, Caesarea

160 SILENT PRAYER. 1942.
Oil on canvas, 46 × 35 ½".
Collection Mr. and Mrs. Artur Rubinstein,
New York and Paris

161 SELF-PORTRAIT. 1940.
Oil on canvas, 14 × 10 ½″.
Collection Dr. Cécile Segal, Paris

162 *(right)* ESTHER. 1943.
Oil on canvas, 26 × 20″.
Collection Esther Rubin, Tel Aviv

163 SUNFLOWERS. 1942.
Oil on canvas, 39 × 29″.
Collection Mr. and Mrs. Leon Gildesgame,
Mt. Kisco, N.Y.

164 STILL LIFE ON A PINK TABLE. 1943. Oil on canvas, 22 × 34″.
Collection Ariella Rubin, Tel Aviv

165 PEACHES AND CHERRIES. 1940.
Oil on canvas, 8 ½ × 16 ½".
Collection Dr. and
Mrs. H. Weinstock, New York

166 POMEGRANATES. 1942.
Oil on canvas, 10 ½ × 17".
Collection Baronne Alix
de Rothschild, Paris

167 CAMELS AT REST. 1941.
Pen and ink and wash, 12 × 16″.
Collection Mr. and Mrs. A. S. Epstein,
Beverly Hills, Calif.

168 HORSE RACING. 1941.
Pen and ink and wash, 19 × 25″.
Hadassa Klachkin Gallery, Tel Aviv

169 BOUQUET IN A PERSIAN VASE. 1944.
Oil on canvas, 29 × 26″.
Collection Mr. and Mrs. José Ferrer,
Beverly Hills, Calif.

170 SHEPHERD. 1950. Oil on canvas, 36 × 28″.
Collection Mr. and Mrs. Leon Feffer, São Paulo, Brazil

171 TIBERIAS FISHERMAN FAMILY. 1946–54. Oil on canvas, 63 ½ × 51″.
Collection Esther Rubin, Tel Aviv

172 ESCAPING HORSE. 1942. Pen and ink and wash, 22 × 30 ½".
Dalzell Hatfield Galleries, Los Angeles

173 DRINKING IN THE DESERT. 1945. Brush and Chinese ink,
19 ½ × 12 ½". Hadassa Klachkin Gallery, Tel Aviv

174 PORTRAIT OF A LADY IN A GREEN HAT.
1943. Oil on canvas, 36 × 29″.
Collection Stella Adler, New York

175 PORTRAIT OF ABRAHAM WALKOWITZ.
1943. Oil on canvas, 32 × 24″.
Collection the artist, Tel Aviv

176 PORTRAIT OF AN ACTOR. 1944.
Oil on canvas, 32 × 23 ½".
Collection Mr. and Mrs. Sam Jaffe,
Beverly Hills, Calif.

177 DAVID. 1948.
Oil on canvas, 12 × 10 ½″.
Collection Mr. and
Mrs. David Rubin,
Tel Aviv

178 "AND JACOB WENT OUT OF BEERSHEBA." 1948.
Pen and ink and wash, 19 × 12".
From Bruce Rogers Bible, 1948.
Collection Mr. and Mrs. N. Bernstein, Dublin

179 ARABIAN HORSES. 1950.
Pen and ink and wash, 25 × 19".
Collection Robert Adam, Paris

180 EIN KAREM. 1951. Oil on canvas, 21 × 29″.
Collection Dr. and Mrs. David Steine,
Nashville, Tenn.

181 SAFED. 1954. Oil on canvas, 29 × 36″.
Collection Mr. and Mrs. Efraim Ilin, Haifa

182 REST ON THE FLIGHT. 1952–65. Oil on canvas, 21 ½ × 29″.
The Art Museum, Princeton University, N.J.

183 FLUTE PLAYER. 1952. Pen and ink and wash, 19 × 12″.
Collection Dr. and Mrs. David Steine, Nashville, Tenn.

184 MAESTRO ARTUR RUBINSTEIN. 1953.
Pencil, 9 ½ × 7″.
Collection Mr. and Mrs. Artur Rubinstein,
New York and Paris

185 JERUSALEM THE GOLDEN. 1946–66. Oil on canvas, 38 × 64″.
Collection Mr. and Mrs. Philip Vogelman, New York

187 MOTHER AND CHILD. 1957. Lithograph, 15 ½ × 18 ½".
Collection Ariella Rubin, Tel Aviv

186 ARIELLA. 1956. Oil on canvas, 12 × 10 ½".
Collection Mr. and Mrs. M. Ahuronee, Rome and Geneva

188 CAMEL DRIVER. 1954. Pen and ink, wash, and pastel, 15 × 25".
Collection Mr. and Mrs. Lessing J. Rosenwald, Jenkintown, Pa.

194

189 MIMOSA AND LUPINE. 1954.
Oil on canvas, 32 × 26″.
Collection Mr. and Mrs. Ben Oakland,
Beverly Hills, Calif.

190 FAMILY OF DONKEYS. 1956. Pen and ink and wash, 20 × 23 ½″. Collection Ariella Rubin, Tel Aviv

191 DIKLA. 1950.
Oil on canvas, 12 ½ × 10 ½".
Collection Mr. and
Mrs. N. Bernstein, Dublin

192 BOUQUET. 1955. Oil on canvas, 29 × 36″.
Collection Mr. and Mrs. Josef Rosensaft, New York

193 CAMELS AND GOATS. 1956.
Pen and ink and wash, 25 × 19″.
Collection Sadye Bronfman, Montreal

194 SHEEP SHEARER. 1955.
Oil on canvas, 46 × 35".
Detroit Institute of Arts

195 SPRING BOUQUET. 1957.
Oil on canvas, 29 × 24″.
Collection Sir Isaac and
Lady Wolfson, London and Rehovot

196 LANDSCAPE IN GALILEE. 1956. Oil on canvas, 23 ½ × 32".
Collection Marshal Tito, Brioni, Yugoslavia

197 NEAR SAFED. 1957. Oil on canvas, 25 ½ × 36".
Collection Admiral and Mrs. Lewis Strauss, Washington, D.C.

198 SPRINGTIME IN GALILEE. 1956. Oil on canvas, 31 ½ × 39 ½".
Collection Mrs. Florence Heifetz, Beverly Hills, Calif.

199 EIN KAREM. 1958. Oil on canvas, 29 × 36".
Collection Mr. and Mrs. Sam Mallach, Buenos Aires

200 MIMOSA. 1957.
Oil on canvas, 36 × 29″.
Collection Sir Marcus and
Lady Sieff, London

201 BOUQUET WITH MIMOSA. 1958.
Oil on canvas, 40 ½ × 30″.
Collection Mr. and Mrs. Raphael Recanati,
New York

202 MUSICIANS OF SAFED. 1957. Oil on canvas, 63 × 38″. Private collection, New York

203 FLUTE PLAYER AND DONKEY. 1958. Pen and ink and wash, 26 × 20″. Collection Mr. and Mrs. Henri Plessner, Paris

204 POMEGRANATES ON MY WINDOW. 1961. Oil on canvas, 24 × 32″.
Collection Mollie Parnis, New York

205 MIMOSA. 1961.
Oil on canvas, 46 × 35".
Collection Israel Museum,
Jerusalem

206 ANEMONES ON MY WINDOW. 1959. Oil on canvas, 32 × 23 ½″.
Collection Mr. and Mrs. Ben Grauer, New York

207 POMEGRANATES ON A TABLE. 1960. Oil on canvas, 29 × 36″.
Collection Mr. and Mrs. Robert Harvey, Harrison, N.Y.

208 POMEGRANATES ON MY WINDOW. 1958. Oil on canvas, 36 × 29″.
Musée National d'Art Moderne, Paris

209 RED POMEGRANATES. 1959. Oil on canvas, 24 × 20″.
Collection Arnold Weissberger, New York

210 FLUTE PLAYER. 1959.
Oil on canvas, 32 × 26″.
Collection Mr. and
Mrs. Heinz Kern, Caracas

211 MIMOSA AND BLACK IRIS. 1961.
Oil on canvas, 40 × 30″.
Collection Sir Isaac and
Lady Wolfson, London and Rehovot

212 BLACK STALLION. 1960. Oil on canvas, 24 × 36″.
Collection Alex J. Weinstein, Croton-on-Hudson, N.Y.

213 BLACK IRIS AND MIMOSA. 1960. Oil on canvas, 32 × 26″.
Collection Mr. and Mrs. John F. Finn, Jr., New York

214 KNEELING FISHERMAN. 1960.
Pen and ink, wash, and pastel, 25 × 19″.
Collection Alex J. Weinstein,
Croton-on-Hudson, N.Y.

215 DREAMER. 1960.
Oil on canvas, 63 × 38″.
Collection Einstein Institute, New York.
Gift of Mr. M. L. Friedman

216 MOTHER AND CHILD. 1962.
Mixed media, 13 × 9 ½″.
Collection the artist, Tel Aviv

219 MADONNA. 1962. Oil on canvas, 36 × 26″.
Collection Hortense Piness, Beverly Hills, Calif.

217 *(top left)* LANDSCAPE IN GALILEE. 1960. Oil on canvas, 26 × 32″.
Collection H. M. the Queen of Holland.
Gift of the late Israeli President Isaac Ben-Zvi

218 *(bottom left)* ANCIENT OLIVE GROVE IN GALILEE. 1961.
Oil on canvas, 26 × 39″.
Collection H. E. Governor Maurice Brasseur of Luxembourg

220 POPPIES AND WHEAT. 1961. Oil on canvas, 36 × 26″.
Collection Mr. and Mrs. Milton Bliss, New Rochelle, N.Y.

221 HOMAGE TO CASALS. 1962. Oil on canvas, 36 × 29″.
Collection Mr. and Mrs. Gerard Oestreicher, New York

222 WHITE LILACS. 1962.
Oil on canvas, 40 × 29 ½″.
Collection Mr. and Mrs. Louis Regenstein,
Atlanta, Ga.

223 THIS IS THE LAND. 1962–64.
Oil on canvas, 57 ½ × 38 ½″.
Petit Palais, Geneva

224 RED CHRYSANTHEMUMS. 1963. Oil on canvas, 39 ½ × 32″.
Collection Mr. and Mrs. M. Gelman, Washington, D.C.

225 LANDSCAPE WITH OLIVE TREES. 1963. Oil on canvas, 21 ½ × 29″.
Collection Dr. and Mrs. Nahum Goldman, Jerusalem

226 ROOSTER. 1963.
Oil on canvas, 36 × 29″.
Collection Mr. and
Mrs. Peter Gilbert, New York

227 BIRTHDAY BOUQUET. 1963.
Oil on canvas, 40 × 30″.
Collection Mr. and
Mrs. Harvey Gilston, Lausanne

228 WHITE ROSES. 1964.
Oil on canvas, 44 × 37″.
Collection Claude Geismar, Paris

229 GLADIOLI. 1964.
Oil on canvas, 36 × 26″.
Collection Dr. and
Mrs. George Wise, Tel Aviv

230 FISHERMAN OF GALILEE. 1963.
Oil on canvas, 36 × 29″.
Collection Esther Rubin, Caesarea

231 ABRAHAM AND THE THREE ANGELS. 1964–69.
Oil on canvas, 36 × 26".
Collection Mr. and Mrs. Louis S. Kaplan,
New York

232 MUSICIANS OF SAFED. 1965.
Oil on canvas, 36 × 29″.
Collection Virginia Steele Scott, Calif.

233 OPEN WINDOW. 1965.
Oil on canvas, 36 × 29″.
Collection Ariella Rubin, Tel Aviv

234 AFTER THE STORM. 1965.
Oil on canvas, 36 × 29″.
The Rubin Museum Foundation

235 WOMAN WITH WHEAT. 1964.
Oil on canvas, 18 ½ × 15 ½".
Collection Mr. and
Mrs. Louis Hamburger,
Franklin, Mich.

236 WOMAN WITH POMEGRANATE.
1965. Oil on canvas, 32 × 26″.
Collection Mr. and
Mrs. D. Feldman, Montreal

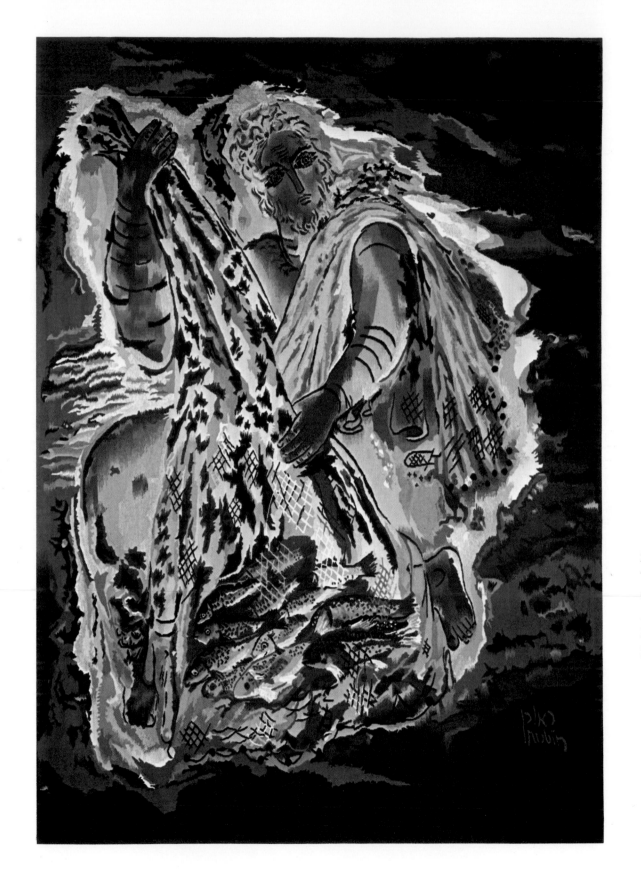

237 LA PÊCHE MIRACULEUSE. 1966.
Tapestry, 106 × 75″.
Collections Mr. and Mrs. Bernard Bloomfield, Montreal;
Mr. and Mrs. Melvin Gelman, Washington, D.C.;
Mr. and Mrs. W. B. Herman, Toronto;
Mr. and Mrs. Sol Slatin, New York

238 GLORY OF GALILEE. 1965–66. Oil on canvas, 75 × 120″.
The Knesset, Jerusalem

239 THE SEGRE SISTERS. 1965.
Oil on canvas, 32 × 24″.
Collection Mr. and
Mrs. Lionello Segre, Turin

240 RABBI WITH TORAH. 1966.
Oil on canvas, 36 × 24″.
Collection Mr. and Mrs. Sidney Baer, Philadelphia

241 YOUNG DAVID PLAYING THE HARP.
1965. Oil on canvas, 18 × 15″.
Collection Paul Gallico, Antibes

242 BLUE HORSES IN CAESAREA. 1966. Oil on canvas, 32 × 51″.
Collection Mr. and Mrs. A. N. Haas, Cleveland

243 THE DIVINE SPIRIT RETURNS TO JERUSALEM. 1967.
Oil on canvas, 63 ½ × 45″.
Collection Mr. and Mrs. Bernard Deutsch, New York

244 RIDER WITH BOUQUET. 1966. Oil on canvas, 29 ½ × 21".
Collection Mr. and Mrs. Max Schein, Mexico City

245 BIBLICAL VISION. 1967. Oil on canvas, 18 × 15".
Collection Mr. and Mrs. William Haber, New York

246 MOTHER AND CHILD. 1967.
Oil on canvas, 36 × 26″.
Collection Dr. and Mrs. Arthur First, Philadelphia

247 THE DREAM. 1965. Pencil and crayon, 14 ½ × 20″.
Hadassa Klachkin Gallery, Tel Aviv

248 PRAYER FOR PEACE. 1967.
Pen and ink, crayon, and gouache, 25 × 20″.
Collection H. Krongold, Toorak,
Victoria, Australia

249 ROOSTER. 1967.
Pen and ink and wash, 25 × 21″.
Collection the artist, Tel Aviv

250 YEMENITE BRIDE. 1968.
Oil on canvas, 29 × 21 ½″.
Collection Mr. and
Mrs. Martin Horowitz, Los Angeles

251 POPPIES IN THE FIELD. 1965. Oil on canvas, 29 × 36″.
Collection Mrs. J. Myer Schine, New York

252 SPRINGTIME BOUQUET. 1968.
Oil on canvas, 36 × 29″.
Collection Mr. and
Mrs. E. Goldenberg, Lima

253 RIDER WITH BOUQUET. 1967–68.
Oil on canvas, 36 × 29″.
Collection Dr. and
Mrs. Kurt Enoch, New York

254 HARVEST NEAR JERUSALEM. 1968. Oil on canvas, 21 × 29″.
Collection Mr. and Mrs. Gregorio Shapiro, Mexico City

255 LANDSCAPE IN GALILEE. 1969. Oil on canvas, 21 × 29″.
Collection Mr. and Mrs. Simon Selig, Atlanta

256 OLD OLIVE FOREST. 1967. Oil on canvas, 38 × 64″.
The Rubin Museum Foundation

257 JERUSALEM THE GOLDEN. 1967–69. Oil on canvas, 51 × 64″.
The Rubin Museum Foundation

258 BIBLICAL VISION. 1966.
Oil on canvas, 32 × 26″.
Collection Mr. and
Mrs. Charles Gordon, London

259 HARVEST TIME NEAR SAFED. 1967.
Oil on canvas, 26 × 32″.
Collection Marguerite Motte, Geneva

260 EARLY MORNING IN GALILEE. 1968.
Oil on canvas, 21 × 28″.
Goldman Gallery, Haifa

... IN THE SHADOW of THY WING
WILL I MAKE MY REFUGE
UNTIL THESE CALAMITIES
BE OVERPAST...
PSALM LVII...

261 PSALM 57:1. ". . . in the shadow
of Thy wing will I make my refuge,
until these calamities
be overpast . . ." 1967.
Pen and ink and crayon, 25 × 20".
Collection the artist, Tel Aviv

262 sheep shearer. 1968.
Mixed media, 26 × 20″.
Collection Mr. and
Mrs. David Rubin, Caesarea

255

263 VICTORY BOUQUET. 1967.
Oil on canvas, 32 × 26″.
Collection Francine Clore, Paris

264 PORTRAIT OF THE POET SHLONSKY.
1968. Oil on canvas, 40 × 30″.
The Rubin Museum Foundation

257

265 RIDERS IN THE NEGEV. 1968. Lithograph, 20 × 26″.
Published by Pucker-Safrai Gallery, Boston, Mass.

266 KING DAVID ENTERS JERUSALEM. 1968. Mixed media, 16 ½ × 21″.
Collection David Rubin, Tel Aviv

267 HASSIDIC DANCE. 1968. Oil on canvas, 29 × 21 ¼″.
Collection Dr. and Mrs. Arthur First, Philadelphia

268 OLD NIGUN. 1969. Oil on canvas, 24 × 20″.
Goldman Gallery, Haifa

269 ABISHAG THE SHUNAMMITE BEFORE KING DAVID. 1970.
Pen and ink and wash, 13 × 18 ½″.
Collection the artist, Tel Aviv

270 KING DAVID ENTERS JERUSALEM. 1970. Oil on canvas, 18 × 15″.
Rosenfeld Gallery, Tel Aviv

271 JACOB'S DREAM. 1968.
Oil on canvas, 36 × 29″.
Collection Mr. and
Mrs. Bernard Deutsch, New York

272 CROWNING OF THE TORAH.
1968–69. Oil on canvas, 32 × 29″.
Collection Dr. and Mrs.
Ronald Fisher, Bridgeton, N.J.

273 SELF-PORTRAIT WITH
JACOB AND THE ANGEL. 1970.
Oil on canvas, 24 × 20″.
Collection Dr. and
Mrs. Haim Gamzu, Tel Aviv

264

274 FAMILY OF SAFED II. 1970.
Oil on canvas, 36 × 29″.
Collection Joseph S. Wohl, Lawrence, N.Y.

275 POMEGRANATES. 1969. Oil on canvas, 24 × 32″.
O'Hana Gallery, London

276 MUSICAL INTERLUDE. 1969. Oil on canvas, 25 ½ × 36″.
Collection Mr. and Mrs. Edward E. Ginsberg, Cleveland and Caesarea

277 HARVEST. 1969. Pen and ink and crayon, 15 × 21″.
Collection the artist, Tel Aviv

278 FIGHTING ROOSTER. 1969–70. Gouache and pastel, 21 ½ × 31″.
Goldman Gallery, Haifa

279 TWO MUSICIANS. 1970.
Watercolor and pastel, 24 × 19″.
Collection the artist, Tel Aviv

280 ABRAHAM AND THE THREE ANGELS. 1970.
Pen and ink and crayon, 26 ½ × 20″.
Collection the artist, Tel Aviv

281 JACOB'S DREAM. 1970.
Oil on canvas, 46 × 35″.
Collection Mr. and
Mrs. David Wolfson, London

282 BOUQUET WITH CAESAREA RUINS.
1970. Oil on canvas, 42 × 35″.
Collection Mr. and
Mrs. Ben Corson, Philadelphia

283 WHITE HORSES IN CAESAREA. 1970. Oil on canvas, 25 ½ × 36″.
Collection Charles Clore, London

284 GALLOPING HORSES. 1971. Oil on canvas, 51 × 64″.
Collection Mr. and Mrs. George Friedland, Philadelphia

285 JERUSALEM THE GOLDEN. 1971. Oil on canvas, 28 × 36″.
Collection Mr. and Mrs. Harry Meisel, Beverly Hills, Calif.

286 BOUQUET NEAR ROMAN AQUEDUCT.
1969. Oil on canvas, 36 × 29″.
Collection Mr. and
Mrs. André Bollag, Zurich

287 ETUDE FOR DOUBLE PORTRAIT. 1971. Pencil, 15 ½ × 19″.

BIOGRAPHICAL OUTLINE

1893	Born in Galatz, Rumania, on November 13. At age of fourteen drawings and sketches published in local papers and magazines.
1912	Went to Jerusalem. Studied for one year at Bezalel School of Arts and Crafts.
1913–14	Paris. Studied at École des Beaux-Arts and Académie Colarossi.
1915	Italy. Visited museums and art galleries.
1916–18	Rumania. Did various jobs to earn a living.
1919–20	Studio in Czernowitz. Painted pictures with tragic themes, did sculpture, wrote poetry.
1921	First one-man show in New York at Anderson Gallery, sponsored by Alfred Stieglitz.
1922	Returned to Jerusalem. A few months later set up studio in a tent on Tel Aviv sand dunes. Exhibition in Bucharest.
1923	First one-man show in Tel Aviv at the Herzlia High School. Designed stage sets and costumes for *Jacob's Dream* and *Joske Musikant* (Vilna Troupe). Published album of woodcuts, *The God Seekers,* in Tel Aviv. Helped create the Palestine Artists Association.

1924	First artist to hold one-man show in the Tower of David in Jerusalem. Exhibition in Bucharest at Regina Maria Gallery.
1925	First one-man show in Paris at Marcel Bernheim Gallery.
1926	Awarded Lord Plumer Prize for painting *My Family*, shown at the annual general collective exhibition of the Palestine Artists Association and presented to the Tel Aviv Museum.
1927	One-man show in Tel Aviv.
1928	Exhibition in Paris at Druet Gallery. Painting *Village of Sumeil* purchased by French government. Exhibition in New York at Guarino Gallery. Acquisitions by Brooklyn and Newark museums.
1930	Married Esther Davis of New York in Tel Aviv. First one-man show in London at Tooth Gallery. Acquisitions by Manchester Gallery of Art and Ben Ury Society.
1930–31	Exhibition in New York at Montross Gallery. Stage designs for Habimah and Ohel theaters.
1932	Opening of the Tel Aviv Museum with one-man Rubin exhibition.
1936–37	Exhibitions in Jerusalem at Steimatzky Gallery and in Tel Aviv at Bach Gallery.
1938	Second exhibition in London at Tooth Gallery. Exhibition in Jerusalem at Bezalel Museum.
1940–45	Exhibition in New York at Milch Gallery (1940). Acquisition of *Flute Player* by The Museum of Modern Art, New York. Exhibition in Los Angeles at Hatfield Galleries (1941). Acquisition by Los Angeles County Museum. Exhibition in San Francisco at Gumps Gallery (1941). Exhibition in New York at Bignou Gallery (1942). Participated in "Twentieth-Century Portraits" exhibition, The Museum of Modern Art, New York (1942). Exhibition in Los Angeles at Hatfield Galleries (1944). Acquisition by Santa Barbara Museum. Tour exhibition of thirty paintings (1944–46), Oklahoma Art Center, Oklahoma City; Witte Museum, San Antonio, Texas; Philbrook Museum, Tulsa, Okla.; Wichita Art Museum, Kan. First Purchase Prize by San Antonio Museum for *Jerusalem from the Mount of Olives*.
1945	Exhibition in New York at Lilienfeld Gallery. Awarded honorary Doctor of Hebrew Letters degree by the Jewish Institute of Religion in New York. Birth of son, David, in New York.

288 Rubin and his wife, Esther,
with Edward G. Robinson in Israel, 1957

289 Rubin with Artur Rubinstein
at the opening of the Mann Concert Hall
in Tel Aviv, 1958

1946	Returned to Palestine in the spring.
1947	Retrospective exhibition at Tel Aviv Museum.
1948	Stage designs for *Hershele Ostropoler* (Ohel), *Day and Night,* and *Noah* (Habimah).
	Appointed Minister Plenipotentiary to Rumania by the new Israeli government.
1948/1950/	
1952	Exhibited at Venice Biennale.
1950	Returned to Tel Aviv.
1952	Birth of daughter, Ariella, in New York.
1953	Two one-man shows in New York at Grace Borgenicht Gallery: paintings in May; drawings in December.
	Acquisition of *Sheep Shearer* by the Museum of Art, University of Arizona, Tucson.
	Participated in group show, "Seven Painters from Israel," Institute of Contemporary Art, Boston; Carnegie Institute, Pittsburgh; Metropolitan Museum of Art, New York; Albright-Knox Gallery, Buffalo; Baltimore Art Museum; Los Angeles County Museum; Tucson Fine Arts Association; J.L. Hudson Co., Detroit.
1954	One-man shows in Los Angeles at Hatfield Galleries; in Charlotte, N. C., at Mint Museum; in Nashville, Tenn., at Parthenon.
1955	Returned to Israel
	Retrospective exhibition at Tel Aviv Museum.
1957	One-man show in London at O'Hana Gallery.
1958	Participated in group show, "Paintings from Israel," Arts Council of Great Britain, London.
1960	Participated in group show, "Contemporary Art in Israel," Musée National d'Art Moderne, Paris. Acquisition of *Goldfish Vendor* and *Pomegranates on My Window* by museum.
1961	Album of twelve lithographs, *Visages d'Israël,* published by Daniel Jacomet, Paris.
1962	Retrospective exhibition in New York at Wildenstein Galleries.
	Retrospective exhibitions in Los Angeles at Hatfield Galleries, in Tucson at Rosequist Gallery.
1964	Prize of the city of Tel Aviv for lifetime artistic achievement.
1966	*Glory of Galilee* commissioned for the Knesset (parliament), Jerusalem; hung in the Cabinet chamber.
	Retrospective exhibition, Israel

Museum, Jerusalem, and Tel Aviv Museum.

First one-man show in Switzerland, Galerie Motte, Geneva.

1967 First one-man show in Florida, Norton Gallery of Art, Palm Beach. Acquisition of *Musical Interlude in Caesarea* by museum.

1968 Planting of Rubin Forest in hills of Jerusalem.

1969 Stained-glass window commissioned for new residency of the President of Israel in Jerusalem.

Publication of autobiographical sketches, *My Life, My Art*.

1970 Executed portfolio of twelve lithographs, *The Story of King David*, for XXe Siècle, Paris; made drawings for twelve lithographs, *The Prophets,* for Transworld Art Corp., New York; made drawings for twelve lithographs, *Visions of the Bible,* for Harry N. Abrams, Inc., New York.

1971 Artist-of-the-year award, University of Judaism, Los Angeles.

Executed "Bird of Peace" jewelry design for Cartier, New York.

290 Rubin with Israeli Prime Minister Golda Meir, 1968

291 In David Ben-Gurion's library, Tel Aviv; Rubin presenting his book, *My Life, My Art,* to the statesman on his eighty-fifth birthday, 1971

292 Rubin and Esther presenting the new President of the State of Israel, Professor Efraim Katzir, with the portfolio *The Prophets,* 1973

BIBLIOGRAPHY

BOOKS

Fischer, Yona.   *Art in Israel,* edited by B. Tammuz and M. Wykes-Joyce, pp. 18, 19–20. Tel Aviv: Massadah, 1965.

Fleg, Edmond.   *Ma Palestine,* pp. 169–73. Paris: Rieder, 1932.

Gamzu, Haim.   *Painting and Sculpture in Israel,* pp. 15, 19, 33–34. Tel Aviv: Eshcol, 1951.

Kolb, Eugene.   *Jewish Art,* edited by Cecil Roth, pp. 906, 908–9. Tel Aviv: Massadah, 1961.

Newman, Elias.   *Art in Palestine,* pp. 10, 90. New York: Siebel, 1939.

Rubin, Reuven.   *My Life, My Art.* New York: Funk and Wagnalls, Sabra Books, 1969.

St. John, Robert.   *Shalom Means Peace,* pp. 262–66. New York: Doubleday, 1949.

Schwarz, Karl.   *Modern Jewish Art in Israel,* pp. 70, 72, 100. Jerusalem: Reuben Mass, 1941. In Hebrew.

_____.   *Jewish Artists of the 19th and 20th Centuries,* pp. 258–60. New York: Philosophical Library, 1949.

Werner, Alfred.   *Rubin.* Tel Aviv: Massadah, 1958.

Wilkinson, Sarah.   *The Rebirth of Israel,* edited by Israel Cohen, pp. 299, 302. London: E. Goldston, 1952.

Zartel, Moshe.   *Jewish Artists,* pp. 131–32. Tel Aviv: Sifriat Poalim (Workers' Library), 1970. In Hebrew.

PERIODICALS

Banin, Sylvia Satten.   "Rubin: Artist of Israel," *Wizo Review* (Tel Aviv), May–June 1970.

Bialik, Chaim Nachman. "The Painter Rubin," *Moznaim* (Tel Aviv), February 1927. In Hebrew.

———. "The Painter Rubin," *Hasmonaea* (Bucharest), May–June 1927. In Rumanian.

Bickel, Shlomo. "The Painter Rubin," *Di Goldene Ket* (Tel Aviv), May 1966. In Yiddish.

Blakestone, Oswell. "Israeli Artist at the O'Hana," *Apollo* (London), June 1957.

———. "Works from Israel," *Art News* (New York), 8 June 1957.

Coates, Robert M. "Galleries: Rubin," *New Yorker,* 23 June 1953.

Cohen, B. H. "Un Peintre raconte sa vie," *Israelitisches Wochenblatt* (Zurich), 10 April 1970.

Comay, Joan. "Artist and Diplomat Reuven Rubin," *Israel Speaks* (New York), July 1950.

Domingos, Gilberto. "Reuben Rubin," *Brazil-Israel* (São Paulo), August 1956. In Portuguese.

Faerber, Meir. "Ueber 40 Yahre Maler Rubin," *Der Neue Israel* (Zurich), July 1955. In German.

Fineman, Irving. "A Painter's Palestine," *New Palestine* (New York), 10 August 1928.

———. "Rubin: Painter of Peace," *National Jewish Monthly* (Washington, D.C.), June 1941.

Friedman, D. A. "Rubin," *Moznaim* (Tel Aviv), February 1937. In Hebrew.

Gainsborough, Ralph. "Portrait of the Artist Rubin," *Art News and Review* (London), 25 May 1957.

Gamzu, Haim. "Rubin," *Di Goldene Ket* (Tel Aviv), July 1970. In Yiddish.

Gutman, Nahum. "Reuven Rubin," *Davar Leyeladim* (Tel Aviv), 24 December 1963. In Hebrew.

Hellman, George S. "Rubin the Palestinian," *American Hebrew* (New York), 7 November 1930.

———. "Palestine's Gauguin," *Menorah Journal* (New York), November 1930.

Herzog, Aura. "Rubin: Doyen of Israeli Artists," *Jewish Chronicle* (London), 3 August 1962.

Katz, Isaac. "Introduction à l'évolution de l'art pictural en Eretz Israel," *Illustration Juive* (Alexandria, Egypt), December 1929.

Katznelson, Rifka. "Rubin the Painter," *Davar Hapoelet* (Tel Aviv), April 1970. In Hebrew.

Lowenthal, Marvin. "Rubin, a Drawing in Washable Colours," *Israel Life and Letters* (New York), March 1953.

Maizel, N. "Rubin," *Literarishe Bleter* (Warsaw), June 1936. In Yiddish.

Patai, Edith. "Rubin," *Mult es Jovo* (Budapest), March 1931.

_____. "Rubin: Tel Aviv Festoje," *Mult es Jovo* (Budapest), July 1939.

Plaut, James S. "Seven Painters of Israel," *Israel Life and Letters* (New York), January 1953.

Reed, Judith Kaye. "Rubin, Returning to Israel, Holds Exhibition," *Art Digest* (New York), 1 May 1947.

Reiss, Jacques. "Le Peintre de la poesie d'Israël," *Amitiés France-Israël* (Paris), November 1961.

Rubin, Reuven. "I Find Myself," *Menorah Journal* (New York), October 1926.

Salzman, Dorit. "The Artist Rubin," *Davar Leyeladim* (Tel Aviv), 23 April 1968. In Hebrew.

Schack, William. "Rubin," *The Studio* (London), August 1928.

_____. "Rubin," *Creative Art* (New York), August 1928.

_____. "Rubin," *Menorah Journal* (New York), December 1928.

_____. "Israeli Painting After 25 Years," *Commentary* (New York), June 1953.

Shafran, F. "Rubin the Painter," *Freiheit* (New York), December 1942. In Yiddish.

Tal, Miriam. "Rubin Retrospective," *Gazith Art and Literary Journal* (Tel Aviv), June 1966. In Hebrew.

Talphir, Gabriel. "Rubin: Forty Years of Creation," *Gazith Art and Literary Journal* (Tel Aviv), June–July 1955. In Hebrew.

_____. "Reuven Rubin," *Gazith Art and Literary Journal* (Tel Aviv), February 1966. In Hebrew.

Van Vriesland-Hoofien, J. "Palestine Comes to America," *Hadassah Newsletter* (New York), July 1940.

Weinberg, Bernard. "Troubadour pictural d'Israël," *Amitiés France-Israël* (Paris), October 1955.

Weinberg, Mia. "Wedding at Six in the Morning," *La Isha* (Tel Aviv), 31 May 1970. In Hebrew.

Werner, Alfred. "Rubin, Painter and Diplomat," *American Hebrew* (New York), 10 February 1950.

_____. "A Feast of Colour: A Pen Sketch of Reuben Rubin," *New Palestine* (New York), June 1950.

_____. "Diplomat-Artist Retires to Painters' Paradise," *Zionist Record* (Johannesburg), 4 August 1950.

_____. "Gauguin of Israel," *Jewish Affairs* (Johannesburg), July 1951.

_____. "The Magic World of Rubin," *Israel Life and Letters* (New York), October 1952.

_____. "Representative Artists," *Israel Life and Letters* (New York), January 1953.

_____. "Painting the Glory of Palestine," *Reconstructionist* (New York), 29 June 1956.

_____. "Reuben Rubin at Seventy," *Jewish Heritage* (Washington, D.C.), Fall 1963.

_____. "Reuben Rubin: Pioneer of Israeli Art," *Arts* (New York), August 1968.

_____. "Reuben Rubin: Pioneer of Israeli Art," *Women's American Art Reporter* (New York), May–June, 1970.

Wilkinson, Sarah. "Rubin," *Jewish Affairs* (Johannesburg), December 1947.

_____. "The Palette of a Poet," *Ariel: Review of the Arts and Sciences in Israel* (Jerusalem), no. 13, 1966.

_____. "La Palette d'un poète," *Amitiés France-Israël* (Paris), February 1967.

Yanai, J. "Rubin: 'Visages d'Israël,'" *Gazith Art and Literary Journal* (Tel Aviv), April–May 1961. In Hebrew.

CATALOGUES

BOSTON

Institute of Contemporary Art. "Seven Painters from Israel." Foreword by James S. Plaut. 1953.

CHARLOTTE, N.C.

Mint Museum of Art. "Rubin." Foreword by Bruce St. John. 1954.

GENEVA

Galerie Motte. "Rubin." Introduction by Haim Gamzu. 1966.

JERUSALEM

Israel Museum. "Rubin Retrospective." Introduction by Haim Gamzu. 1966.

_____. "Migdal David: Beginnings of Painting in Eretz Israel." Foreword by Yona Fischer. 1968.

Steimatzky Gallery. "Group Exhibition." 1933.

_____. "Rubin." 1934.

_____. "Rubin." 1936.

Tower of David. "Reuven Rubin." Introduction by R. Benjamin. 1924.

LONDON

Arts Council of Great Britain. "Painting from Israel." Preface by Philip James. Introduction by Karl Katz. 1958.

O'Hana Gallery. "Rubin: Recent Paintings and Drawings." Foreword by Eric Newton. 1957.

Sir Arthur Tooth and Sons. "Rubin." 1930.

LOS ANGELES

Dalzell Hatfield Galleries. "Rubin." 1941.

_____. "Contrasts: Six Painters." 1942.

_____. "Rubin." 1944.

_____. "Rubin." 1954.

_____. "Rubin: Fiftieth Anniversary Exhibition." 1962.

NEW YORK

Bignou Gallery. "Recent Paintings by Rubin." 1942.

Grace Borgenicht Gallery. "Rubin: Paintings." Foreword by James S. Plaut. 1953.

_____. "Rubin: Drawings." 1953.

Guarino Gallery. "Rubin." Foreword, "Rubin: Painter of Palestine," by George S. Hellman. 1928.

Metropolitan Museum of Art. "Seven Painters from Israel." Foreword by James S. Plaut. 1953.

Milch Gallery. "Rubin: Recent Paintings." Foreword by Marie Sterner. 1940.

Montross Gallery. "Rubin." Foreword, "Gauguin of Palestine," by George S. Hellman. 1930.

The Museum of Modern Art. "Twentieth-Century Portraits." Preface by Monroe Wheeler. 1942.

Wildenstein Galleries. "Rubin." 1962.

PALM BEACH

Norton Gallery. "Reuven Rubin." Foreword by Haim Gamzu. 1967.

PARIS

Galerie Marcel Bernheim. "Rubin." Foreword by Edmond Fleg. 1925.

Galerie Druet. "Rubin." 1928.

Musée National d'Art Moderne. "L'Art israëlien contemporain." Foreword by Jean Cassou. Introduction by F. Schiff. 1960.

PITTSBURGH

Carnegie Institute. "Seven Painters from Israel." Foreword by James S. Plaut. 1953.

TEL AVIV

Bach Gallery. "Rubin." 1936.

Rothschild Boulevard. "Rubin." Introduction by Haim Nachman Bialik. 1927.

Sherman Art Gallery. "Opening Exhibition." Foreword by M. Sherman. 1946.

Tel Aviv Museum. "Rubin." 1947.

_____. "Rubin Retrospective: Forty Years of Painting Israel." Foreword by Eugene Kolb. 1955.

_____. "Israel Art in Its Beginnings." Introduction by Eugene Kolb. 1957.

_____. "Rubin Retrospective." Introduction by Haim Gamzu. 1966.

VENICE

Venice Biennale. "Paintings from Israel." Introduction by Eugene Kolb. 1952.

PHOTOGRAPH CREDITS

The author and publisher wish to thank the museums, public institutions, and private collectors for permitting the reproduction of works in their collections. The photographs in this book have been provided by the artist with the exception of the following, whose courtesy is gratefully acknowledged:

Oliver Baker, New York: 142, 156; Geoffrey Clements, New York: 143; Colten Photos, New York: 135, 148, 149, 151, 157, 161, 166, 174–176; Davis Dunlop, Washington, D.C.: 128; Photo Erde-Efraim Erde, Tel Aviv: 16, 18, 39, 55, 56, 76, 94; Ran Erde, Tel Aviv: 3; David Harris, Jerusalem: 102; Joseph Leor, Tel Aviv: 290; Izhak Moses, Tel Aviv: 5, 58, 73; Arnold Newman, New York: 31; Riwkin, Stockholm: 74, 75; Roas Photo, Jerusalem: 292; M. Routhier, Paris: 179; John D. Schiff, New York: 180, 183; Photo Sternberg, Israel: 288; Marc Vaux, Paris: 97; I. Zafrir, Tel Aviv: 19, 21, 23–26, 28, 30, 33, 34, 36, 52–54, 57, 77–82, 84–93, 95, 100, 101, 105–108, 111–113, 115–117, 120–124, 126, 127, 129, 132, 133, 136, 137, 140, 141, 152, 155, 160, 162, 169, 170, 171, 173, 177, 181, 182, 184, 186–189, 192, 193, 196–200, 202, 207–209, 212–214, 217–221, 224, 226, 229, 230, 233, 236, 239, 240, 243–245, 259, 260, 263, 264, 267–270, 273, 286